Getting Started with Spiceworks

Install, configure, and get real results from Spiceworks in just a couple of hours

Darren Schoen

Nitish Kumar

[PACKT] open source ✳

community experience distilled

PUBLISHING

BIRMINGHAM - MUMBAI

Getting Started with Spiceworks

Copyright © 2013 Packt Publishing

First published: August 2013

Production Reference: 1160813

Published by Packt Publishing Ltd.
Livery Place
35 Livery Street
Birmingham B3 2PB, UK.

ISBN 978-1-78216-684-9

www.packtpub.com

Cover Image by Suresh Mogre (suresh.mogre.99@gmail.com)

Credits

Authors
Darren Schoen
Nitish Kumar

Acquisition Editor
Kunal Parikh

Commissioning Editor
Sruthi Kutty

Technical Editors
Ruchita Bhansali
Amit Ramadas
Pragati Singh
Aniruddha Vanage

Copy Editors
Gladson Monteiro
Sayanee Mukherjee
Adithi Shetty
Laxmi Subramanian

Project Coordinator
Amigya Khurana

Proofreader
Katherine Tarr

Indexer
Monica Ajmera Mehta

Production Coordinator
Adonia Jones

Cover Work
Adonia Jones

About the Authors

Darren Schoen has always been passionate about technology. He realized this the first time he logged into Prodigy with his DeskPro (through DOS of course). He has come a long way since those amber screens. Although he spent 16 years in another career, in 2001 he decided to pursue this passion and jumped into the IT field. Today, he is the Director of Technology Infrastructure at Broward Center for the Performing Arts in Ft Lauderdale, FL along with being an official Spice Trainer where he travels around the U.S. educating users on Spiceworks. He is on the board of several organizations, always keeping technology and innovation in focus. If that doesn't keep him busy enough, he is also an active speaker around the U.S. and has written a variety of blogs and articles for many publications. Darren is always plugged in, but when he gets some free cycles, he is known to be an avid gamer, a Doctor Who fan, and enjoys reading Hugh Howey and watching live music. Although technology is his life, he does take time out to watch the moon rise on the beach with his wife, Thais, and walk his Boston Terrier, Rocky.

First and foremost, I would like to thank my wife, Thais, for her unconditional support and understanding while I was writing this book. Next, I would like to thank my family, who has always encouraged me to pursue my wildest dreams, no matter how crazy they sounded at times! I wish to also thank my contacts at Packt Publishing: Amigya Khurana and Ameya Sawant, along with my co-author Nitish Kumar, for such an amazing experience while writing this book. I would like to thank my friends and associates who understood when I had to devote time to this project: Dave Schleuter, Tim Weeks, Ricky Lawton, Peter Sze, and Ruth Hinds.

I want to also thank every user or presenter I have come into contact with the past few years, whether I was attending, presenting, or educating, I have learned something from every one of you.

Lastly, I want to thank everyone at Spiceworks and Spiceworks
University because if they didn't create this awesome piece
of software, this book would not be possible; the founders of
Spiceworks, Scott Abel, Jay Hallberg, Francis Sullivan, and Greg
Kattawar; the incredible team at Spiceworks itself (and these are only
a few): Jen Slaski, Nicole Tanzillo, Ashley Connell, Jessica Noland,
Raychelle Geggatt, Sheryl Floyd, and Todd Dorroca, and the great
team of Spice Trainers that have taught me so much, including Bob
Beatty, Grey Howe, Justin Davidson, and Philip Moya.

Nitish Kumar is a Wintel Lead at HT Media Ltd. and an independent tech blogger
about various technologies. He has been working on several Microsoft technologies
and open source solutions (including but not limited to Spiceworks, ManageEngine
Products, Zabbix, MS Active Directory, MS Exchange Servers, and so on) for the
past eight years, of which the last couple of years have been spent on bringing
cost-effective solutions to corporates to simplify their complex requirements and
to improve time management for their staff. He is a technology enthusiast and has
been an active participant at various corporate events and public webinars. Mobile
technologies have been of special interest to him and he has often written about
various gadgets and their respective technologies. Nitish holds an MS degree in
Software from the JK Institute of Applied Physics and Technology, and his areas of
interest include Microsoft technologies, open source software, and mobile gadgets.
He occasionally blogs at http://nitishkumar.net and can be reached over e-mail
at nitish@nitishkumar.net.

A huge thanks to my wife, Pooja, and colleagues for being there, and
to my kiddo for enduring through the process of writing this book.
Of course, thanks to the whole Spiceworks team and community,
especially Jason himself for helping me out for smaller details; this
book would not exist without them. Thanks to the team at Packt
Publishing for their persistence and patience; it surely was hard to
work with a chaotic person like me.

www.PacktPub.com

Support files, eBooks, discount offers and more

You might want to visit www.PacktPub.com for support files and downloads related to your book.

Did you know that Packt offers eBook versions of every book published, with PDF and ePub files available? You can upgrade to the eBook version at www.PacktPub.com and as a print book customer, you are entitled to a discount on the eBook copy. Get in touch with us at service@packtpub.com for more details.

At www.PacktPub.com, you can also read a collection of free technical articles, sign up for a range of free newsletters and receive exclusive discounts and offers on Packt books and eBooks.

http://PacktLib.PacktPub.com

Do you need instant solutions to your IT questions? PacktLib is Packt's online digital book library. Here, you can access, read and search across Packt's entire library of books.

Why Subscribe?

- Fully searchable across every book published by Packt
- Copy and paste, print and bookmark content
- On demand and accessible via web browser

Free Access for Packt account holders

If you have an account with Packt at www.PacktPub.com, you can use this to access PacktLib today and view nine entirely free books. Simply use your login credentials for immediate access.

Table of Contents

Preface

Automated network inventory, full self-service help desk, robust reporting, system monitoring and alerts, Mobile Device Management, software and warranty tracking and inventory, dynamic network map and knowledge base, and also the vibrant online community to share/download content and tools are some of the features on system administrators' and IT pros' wish list, which will help them automate and make their daily tasks more efficient. There is a single product that over two million IT pros have installed that does all these and more. No more separate data silos where you have to export/import to see a comprehensive overview. No more having to manually monitor an e-mail box to track user issues. No more installing clients throughout your network to collect even the most basic information from your desktops and servers. If you are struggling with any or all of these challenges, Spiceworks is your solution.

This book provides a walkthrough from installation to configuration of all these topics and more. The screenshots illustrate important areas of the application and guides you throughout. In only an afternoon, you can traverse installation, network inventory, help desk, reporting, and more with the result being a fully functioning and powerful installation of Spiceworks providing you with important data.

One last thing, Spiceworks does all this for free. Yes, you read that right, absolutely free.

So, come along and find out what over two million IT pros already know, that Spiceworks is an essential enterprise tool that no organization should be without. Come join the Spiceworks IT revolution.

What this book covers

Chapter 1, Setting Up Spiceworks, starts off with an overview of all aspects of the Spiceworks application. Then, we go through a step-by-step process of downloading and installing Spiceworks on your network.

Chapter 2, Configuring Network Inventory in Spiceworks, covers setting up of Spiceworks to scan your network, including best practices and Active Directory configuration.

Chapter 3, Configuring the Spiceworks Help Desk and User Portal, provides a detailed, step-by-step instruction on how to set up the Spiceworks Help Desk and self-serve User Portal. Customization of both the portal and help desk tickets are also covered.

Chapter 4, Configuring Other Spiceworks Features, talks about additional features in Spiceworks, such as Reporting, System monitoring and alerts, Mobile Device Management, Dynamic Network Map, Knowledge base, and Cloud services dashboard.

Chapter 5, Taking Spiceworks to the Next Level, tells you how to take things to the next level by leveraging the vibrant Spiceworks community to gain knowledge and interact with fellow IT Pros.

What you need for this book

You will need an open mind for this book. Throw out any preconceived notions you have about "free software" and look at Spiceworks for what it does well.

Here is what you will need:

- OS requirements:
    - Windows XP Professional SP2 or later
    - Windows Vista
    - Windows 7
    - Windows 2003 Server SP1 or later
    - Windows 2008 Server

- Browser requirements:
    - The latest version of Mozilla Firefox
    - The latest version of Google Chrome
    - Internet Explorer 7.0 or later
    - Safari

- E-mail server requirements:
    - IMAP/POP/SMTP
    - Exchange 2003/2007/2010

Who this book is for

This book is for system administrators, IT pros, help desk technicians, IT directors, multiservice providers, and anyone else who wants to make their IT life easier.

Conventions

In this book, you will find a number of styles of text that distinguish between different kinds of information. Here are some examples of these styles, and an explanation of their meaning.

Code words in text are shown as follows: "As you can see, if you need to put device-specific usernames and passwords into Spiceworks, you can by using the format, `Domain\username`."

Any command-line input or output is written as follows:

```
netstat -a | find "80"
```

New terms and **important words** are shown in bold. Words that you see on the screen, in menus or dialog boxes for example, appear in the text like this: "Clicking on **Language Packs** brings up the multitude of different ones that users have completed."

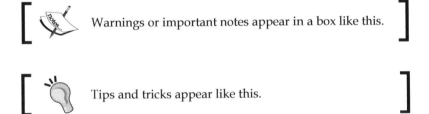

Warnings or important notes appear in a box like this.

Tips and tricks appear like this.

Reader feedback

Feedback from our readers is always welcome. Let us know what you think about this book—what you liked or may have disliked. Reader feedback is important for us to develop titles that you really get the most out of.

To send us general feedback, simply send an e-mail to `feedback@packtpub.com`, and mention the book title via the subject of your message.

If there is a topic that you have expertise in and you are interested in either writing or contributing to a book, see our author guide on `www.packtpub.com/authors`.

Customer support

Now that you are the proud owner of a Packt book, we have a number of things to help you to get the most from your purchase.

Errata

Although we have taken every care to ensure the accuracy of our content, mistakes do happen. If you find a mistake in one of our books—maybe a mistake in the text or the code—we would be grateful if you would report this to us. By doing so, you can save other readers from frustration and help us improve subsequent versions of this book. If you find any errata, please report them by visiting http://www.packtpub. com/submit-errata, selecting your book, clicking on the **errata submission form** link, and entering the details of your errata. Once your errata are verified, your submission will be accepted and the errata will be uploaded on our website, or added to any list of existing errata, under the Errata section of that title. Any existing errata can be viewed by selecting your title from http://www.packtpub.com/support.

Piracy

Piracy of copyright material on the Internet is an ongoing problem across all media. At Packt, we take the protection of our copyright and licenses very seriously. If you come across any illegal copies of our works, in any form, on the Internet, please provide us with the location address or website name immediately so that we can pursue a remedy.

Please contact us at copyright@packtpub.com with a link to the suspected pirated material.

We appreciate your help in protecting our authors, and our ability to bring you valuable content.

Questions

You can contact us at questions@packtpub.com if you are having a problem with any aspect of the book, and we will do our best to address it.

1
Setting Up Spiceworks

Welcome to the wonderful, crazy world of Spiceworks! For those of you who don't know what exactly Spiceworks is, it is a free application for IT professionals (like you and me). It brings together many of the tasks that we do on an everyday basis and consolidates them into a single interface. Oh, did I mention it was free? Yes, free!. Spiceworks was started in 2006 by four veterans of the IT software business. They wanted to bring IT pros a tool that would make their jobs easier and give it away for nothing. That was a huge challenge, but seven years later Spiceworks has over two million users and is installed in every country on the planet. A lot has changed since 2006 and Spiceworks Beta. Let's go through a high-level overview of some of what Spiceworks actually delivers today:

- **Network inventory**: Spiceworks scans your network, extracting information from workstations, servers, network devices (switches, routers), printers, and virtualization hosts. Installed software, updates, and essential information that an IT pro needs at a glance is collected.

- **Integrated help desk/user portal**: Spiceworks has a full-featured help desk integrated within the app so that you can associate issues, devices, and even purchases on one interface. Not only is it useful to the IT pro for setting tasks within a team, it has a front-facing portal so your users can submit their own tickets (and check on the status of the open tickets).

- **Robust reporting**: We all know that information is only as good as the method; we have to get it into a usable form. Spiceworks brings a strong reporting structure so not only will you be able to get those reports, but you will also be able to schedule automatic reports and create your own either using the interface or direct SQL commands.

- **Purchasing**: Need a quote on a piece of equipment? Need to track exactly when something was bought and when it needs to be replaced? Need to know exactly when a piece of equipment is off warranty and, therefore, needs to be replaced? Spiceworks has all this covered. Even if you need several quotes for a single purchase, Spiceworks can get that for you in a few clicks.

- **Community**: The Spiceworks application is integrated with the Spiceworks online community that has over two million members. Ask questions, get answers, find reviews from fellow IT pros, and see how they address the challenges they face. Find that specific report you are looking for and share the report you just created. You can even find local Spiceworks user groups (called SpiceCorps) and meet IT pros in your neck of the woods.

- **Plugins**: Spiceworks brings so many great things right out of the box. Having said that, there are no two IT infrastructures alike. There are literally hundreds of user-created plugins that can customize Spiceworks to your needs.

- **So much more**: Integrated knowledge base, dynamic network map, monitoring, alerts, warranty, and asset tracking are other features that Spiceworks brings out of the box. In addition, new features are being integrated in every new release with many of those chosen by the Spiceworks users themselves.

Since this is a Getting Started book, we will be going over each of these areas in broad strokes with the result being, you having a working and fully-functional Spiceworks installed. Here is what you can expect from this book:

- Getting Spiceworks installed and logging into the Spiceworks Community

- Setting up network inventory and scans

- Setup and configuration of your help desk

- Other Spiceworks features: reporting, monitoring, alerts, purchasing, knowledge base, and others

- Taking Spiceworks to the next level with the Spiceworks Community

So are you ready to install Spiceworks and get this great Spicy stuff on your network? Let's jump right in!

Installing Spiceworks

First we need a machine to install Spiceworks on. Overall it is a pretty lightweight application with minimum system requirements as follows:

- Operating system:
    - Windows 7
    - Windows XP Professional SP2 or later
    - Windows Vista
    - Windows 2003 Server SP1 or later
    - Windows 2008 Server

- Hardware:
    - 1.5 GHz Pentium 4 Class Processor (Minimum)
    - 2.0 GB RAM (Minimum)

- A decommissioned server, a spare desktop, or even a virtual machine. As long as it has network connectivity any of these can work as a Spiceworks host.

 A Spiceworks install works well in virtual environments. Just spin up a virtual machine, install one of the mentioned operating systems, and you are good to go.

Once our Spiceworks host is ready, we now have to download the install package. Simply open your browser and type:

```
www.spiceworks.com/packt
```

The install package is just 60 MB. Navigate to where you want the file to be downloaded to, and then click on Save. Once the Spiceworks package download is complete, double-click on it to start the install process.

 IIS does not need to be installed on the Windows machine you are working on because during the install Spiceworks installs its own IIS.

The Spiceworks install is pretty straightforward. It includes installation of all web components, the database, and the infrastructure that makes the app run. The first screen you will see gives you the option of what port you want to run Spiceworks on (default is port **80**). If you already have any kind of web server running on the machine which you are installing Spiceworks on, this will give you the opportunity to configure it so you do not have any conflicts.

Once you have set the port, click on **Next**. **Terms and Conditions** follow the port assignment window. Read the terms and conditions if you wish to, click on the **Accept** radio button, and click on **Next**. The next window you will see gives you the option to change **Destination Folder** for the install. Initially, Spiceworks needed around 120 MB for the install. This does include a blank database that it will use to store all help desk tickets, network inventory, and reports. Expect this to grow as you use Spiceworks, although not exponentially. If you initially have 1 GB of space, that should be adequate.

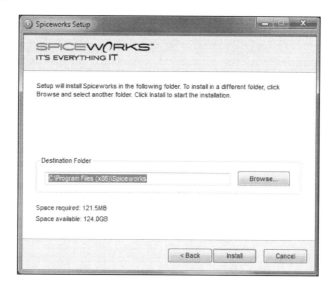

On computers running a 64-bit operating system, Spiceworks is installed in the (x86) directory. Spiceworks works equally well on 32- or 64-bit operating systems.

Once the port has been set, terms and conditions have been accepted, and the destination folder is defined, Spiceworks will begin installing. Since Spiceworks is a web-based application, this process should not take too long. On most machines, initial install usually takes around five minutes (depending on hardware, it could take longer if the machine is closer to the minimum hardware requirements).

When Spiceworks has finished its first phase of installation, the following screen will appear signifying that all components of Spiceworks are now on your system.

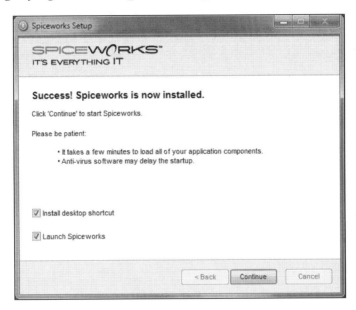

Since this was so quick and easy, let's just check both the boxes and click on the **Continue** button to start the second phase of Spiceworks installation. If you want to continue the install at a later time, just uncheck the **Start Spiceworks** box (but leave the **Create Shortcut on Desktop** box checked), and hit **Continue**. The second phase of installation/configuration does take longer than the initial install, depending on the amount of resources on the machine. This phase configures and loads the application components, and configures the local database.

If you have either chosen to continue the install immediately or come back to it at a later time, the process will be the same when you initially start Spiceworks. First the Spiceworks web server will start and then your default web browser will open to the following screen:

As stated, this process will normally take longer than the initial installation. There are tabs for you to learn about the different areas of Spiceworks, most are videos and quite funny. You might as well get a laugh while you wait! Spiceworks is now configuring all application components, setting up the local database for use, and finalizing configuration of all modules so you can get going on all the spicy goodness that it brings.

This configuration process can take as little as 5 minutes or as long as 30 minutes depending on resources and the configuration of the machine Spiceworks is installed on.

Okay, while we are waiting on this phase to complete, let's get into some of the nuts and bolts about Spiceworks. One of the great things about Spiceworks is that it is pretty much a stand-alone application. It does not have many dependencies on the OS. This is fantastic in a couple of ways. First, as an IT pro, you don't have to put in a ton of work to get a machine ready for Spiceworks. A simple, vanilla install of one of the supported operating systems is all you need. Second, an IT pro such as yourself doesn't have to worry about updating components of the operating system to keep Spiceworks going. Once you install Spiceworks, you are good to go.

Checking back, once this phase of installation/configuration has completed, you will be presented with the following screen:

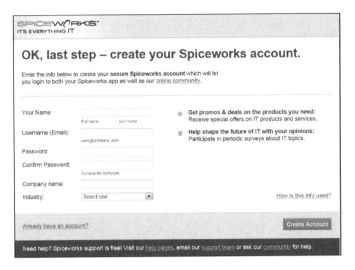

To get to the Spiceworks Desktop (Administrative Interface), every user will need a username and password. You are setting up your first user right now by filling in this information. Put in your name, e-mail address, password, company, and industry, and then click the **Create Account** button. Once you get into Spiceworks, you will not have to input all this information to create other users who will use the application. This is a one-time process.

Once you have created your account, a screen will pop up asking you if you want to set up your inventory, help desk, or configuration. Since we are going to go over these topics a little later in the book, for now, let's just click on the link **look around on your own** at the bottom Don't worry, we will get to these soon enough.

Congratulations! You have successfully installed Spiceworks. As a reward, you should grab yourself a cup of coffee (or tea) and a cookie because cookies are delicious.

Troubleshooting installation issues in Spiceworks

Spiceworks usually installs without a hitch for most users. But we know that no two IT infrastructures are alike so here are a few tips and tricks on troubleshooting a Spiceworks install that doesn't work as planned.

- Spiceworks errors during install! HELP!

  ○ Check any anti-virus programs that may be running on the computer you are trying to install Spiceworks on. There may be a window asking you if you want the install package to make changes that you have to approve.

  ○ Are you running a flavor of Linux or OS X? Sorry, Spiceworks won't run on these operating systems. Spin up a Windows machine (XP SP2, Vista, 7, Server 2003, or Server 2008) and try installing again. (Also, sorry Windows 95 users, you are out of luck if you want to run Spiceworks.)

  ○ Make sure that the user that is logged in has administrative privileges on the machine you are trying to install Spiceworks on.

  ○ You may be having a really bad nightmare; try to imagine flying and if you can, you are dreaming. Think happy thoughts and you will wake up soon and find out that Spiceworks really did install.

- My Spiceworks installation won't start. HELP!

  ○ First, open **Task Manager** and make sure that `Spiceworks.exe` is a process that is running. This is the main process for Spiceworks and if that isn't running, Spiceworks won't show up in the browser.

  ○ If `Spiceworks.exe` is not there, double-click on the desktop shortcut again to restart Spiceworks.

  ○ Check the installed programs in **Control Panel** to make sure Spiceworks is listed as an installed application. If not, it didn't install correctly. Reinstall from the package you downloaded.

  ○ If it is there in the Installed Programs list, uninstall and reinstall Spiceworks.

  ○ You are remotely connected to the wrong machine you installed Spiceworks on, double-check (yes, this is why you saw **Exchange Console** when you logged in).

- `Spiceworks.exe` is running but when I open the browser to the Spiceworks app, nothing shows up. HELP!
  - ○ Easy now, we will get you through this. First check any firewall software you have on your machine. Many firewalls block any sites or ports that are not specifically defined.
  - ○ Double-check the port number you installed Spiceworks with. If another application is using the port you specified for Spiceworks, you will not be able to connect. Here is how you find out and fix:

Open a command prompt and type the following:

```
netstat -a | find "80"
```

(Assuming that 80 is the port that you installed Spiceworks on) If any other program is using that protocol or port, it will be listed.

If there is a program listed, just change the Spiceworks port! Here is how that is done:

  - ○ Right-click on the System Tray icon in the lower-right corner of the screen
  - ○ Click on **Preferences**
  - ○ Change the port number...see, that wasn't so hard!
  - ○ Make sure that the localhost or the machine name of the computer you have installed Spiceworks on, is resolved to a correct IP address. (Localhost should be 127.0.0.1)
  - ○ You are trying to use Netscape 2.0 as your browser. I am sorry to say that Netscape 2.0 is not supported by Spiceworks.

- There is a login screen, is that right? Okay, so you may see a login screen with the Spiceworks logo. Just log in with your username (e-mail address) and the password you set up in the previous step.

That takes care of basic troubleshooting. If you do have any other serious issues not covered here, Spiceworks does provide full support for its product. Yes, a free piece of software does provide free support. Crazy I know. Miracles never do cease, do they? Just open a browser to the following link and browse to the **Getting Started** section:

```
http://community.spiceworks.com/help/Troubleshooting
```

Logging in and setting up Spiceworks Admins

If you have chosen to start Spiceworks immediately after the installation, then you will not have to log in. Spiceworks will open directly to your dashboard. If you have chosen to not open Spiceworks directly after the installation, then just open a browser and type the machine name you installed Spiceworks on and the port number. There will be a login screen, just enter the username (e-mail address) and password you created when installing and you will be logged in.

Let's take a look at the first thing you see once Spiceworks opens, the **Dashboard**. This is the interface you will see every time you log into Spiceworks. It is fully customizable and the dashboard that you will have after using Spiceworks for a while will look very different than the one shown in the following screenshot. Let's have a look at the different components and give you an overview of what each component does.

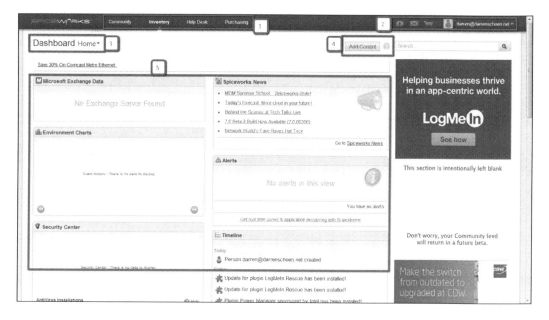

- The area highlighted as **1** shows the navigation bar. Move your cursor onto each option in this bar and you will see the different pages within Spiceworks. We will be hitting on all these—**Community**, **Inventory**, **Help Desk**, **Purchasing**—in this book.

- The area highlighted as **2** shows the notification area. When connected to the community this will show any messages that you have along with alerts from your network inventory and outstanding purchasing quotes you have active. Your username is also here in the top-right corner.

- The area highlighted as **3** shows dashboard information. This tells you what dashboard you are seeing. You can create multiple dashboards that display different types of information, but we will get into that a little later in this chapter.

- The area highlighted as **4** shows the Add Content button. Clicking on this will open up the widget menu and allow you to add different widgets to your dashboard.

- The area highlighted as **5** shows the widget information area Here is where all your widgets are displayed. Right now there isn't much to display as we don't have any data within Spiceworks, but that will be remedied in the next chapter when we set up your network scan.

Whew! That is a LOT of information on one interface. You want to hear something crazy? We haven't even scratched the surface as to what Spiceworks can do yet. Now you should be realizing why more than two million IT pros use this software. Once we get some data from network scans and help desk tickets, we will be revisiting the Dashboard to walk you through customizing it to display the data you need.

Spiceworks users defined

Let's get to know the different types of users in Spiceworks. Here is an overview of each kind and what permissions each one has.

- **Admin**: These users have full administrative privileges within Spiceworks. They can run any report, modify any device within Spiceworks network inventory, and can open, edit, and close any help desk ticket within the application. Only the highest level users should have this access.

- **Help Desk Admin**: These users have full administrative access to the help desk portion of Spiceworks. They cannot change settings, see or modify network scans or inventory, and cannot see or run reports.

- **Help Desk Tech**: These users only have access to help desk tickets that they are either assigned or cc'd on. Like the Help Desk Admin user, they cannot see or modify any of the other aspects of Spiceworks.

- **Reporting**: These users only have access to the reporting portion of Spiceworks. They cannot see or modify any device, help desk ticket, or setting.

We will be going over only the Admin users right now. The help desk users will be covered in *Chapter 3, Configuring the Help Desk and User Portal* and reporting users are covered in *Chapter 4, Configuring Other Spiceworks Features*.

Setting up Spiceworks Admin users

Even if you are going to be the only active Admin on the system, it is always a good idea to set up another user with Admin privileges. One of the reasons is password reset. If you need to reset your password, you can log in as the other user and easily reset it. There is a manual way to reset it as well, but this way is easier! And we are all about things being easy, right? The process is very easy, let's walk through it.

First, mouse over the **Inventory** menu on the top of **Dashboard**. You will see a **Settings** option. Click on it. The option is illustrated as follows:

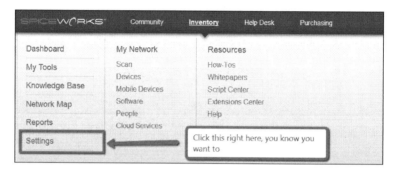

This will take you to the **Settings** page and there is a lot going on here. We will be getting to all these settings, but right now we are only interested in the **Personal** section, specifically the **User Accounts** option. Click on this and it will take you to the **User Accounts** screen. This screen is how we add new users that will use Spiceworks Desktop (in whatever capacity, reporting, help desk, and network inventory).

End users that will use the Spiceworks Help Desk Portal do not need to be added here. Their accounts will automatically be created as they log into the Help Desk Web Portal and they will not need access to the Spiceworks Desktop.

Since you just installed Spiceworks, there should be only one account on this page. The one you created at the last step of installation. There is an **Add** button on the lower-left side below the accounts, just click on it and blank entries for each column will appear.

Enter the e-mail address, the first name, the last name, password, and the user permission level (you won't have to change that as **Admin** is the default setting). Once you have entered all this information in, click on the **Save** button and like magic, a new user is created. See, I told you it would be easy! One more thing to know once the user is created is that an option on whether you choose for this user to receive email notifications will now be visible on the far right side where the **Save** button was. There are four options here. Let's go over what they are.

- **None**: A user receives no e-mail from the Spiceworks app (default).

- **Alerts**: If this box is checked, then any alerts that you set up will be e-mailed out to the user. If this box is the only one checked, the users will not receive any e-mails on Help Desk Tickets or Weekly Summaries.

- **Help Desk**: If this box is checked, then the user will get all notifications on new tickets and also if a ticket has been assigned to them. If you are setting up for either of the Help Desk users (Admin or Tech), this box should be checked.

- **Weekly Updates**: Spiceworks generates weekly updates on what has been added to your network and also some Help Desk analytics. Check this box if you want these to go to the user.

Since we are creating an Admin user, let's just go ahead and mouse over the **None** option under the **Email** column and once the menu bubble comes on the screen, click all the three boxes. There is no Save button. Just move your mouse off the menu and it will be saved automatically. If you know that there are multiple Admin users that you want to add, feel free to do that now. Since we are focusing on Admin users now, we won't worry about creating Help Desk or reporting users so just hold off on those for the moment. What we need to do now is get you logged into the Spiceworks Community.

Getting into the Spiceworks Community

Throughout this book we will be referencing things that are available on the Spiceworks Community. The Community is an integral part of Spiceworks. A place to ask questions, get answers, and also connect with other IT pros and vendors. We go quite in-depth as to what you can find on it in *Chapter 5, Taking Spiceworks to the Next Level* but for right now, let's just get you an account and logged on.

Now, one of the great things about this Community is its tight integration into the app itself. If you look at the top of any of the dashboard pages, the first link on the right is the Community link. If you mouse over it, like any of the other main links in this section of your Spiceworks install, a menu opens up and looks just like the following screenshot:

You can see different categories, resources, and a section devoted to Spiceworks. So let's just click on the **Community** link. A window will pop up that looks like the following screenshot, asking for a username for the Spiceworks community:

Pick a username you want and click on the **Next** button. Your local Spiceworks install will then communicate with the online community to check and see if the username you picked is taken. If it has, Spiceworks will come back to this window with a name suggestion. You can change it if you want to personalize your username, just keep trying different ones or take the suggestion that Spiceworks gives. Don't worry, you can change it later if you wish. Spiceworks then connects to the online community and sets up your profile. The next window that you will see is the following screenshot:

Here is where you can put in as much or as little information as you wish. You can even skip this page if that is what you want to do. Totally up to you. As you get more comfortable in the community and see what it is all about, you will probably put some more information in there so that the other folks know a little about you. Honestly, I was pretty skeptical when I first installed Spiceworks, but now I have my real name, company name, and other non-sensitive information on my Spiceworks profile.

So whether you put in your information or not, the next step is the same. The following window pops up and you are given a series of choices about your IT interests:

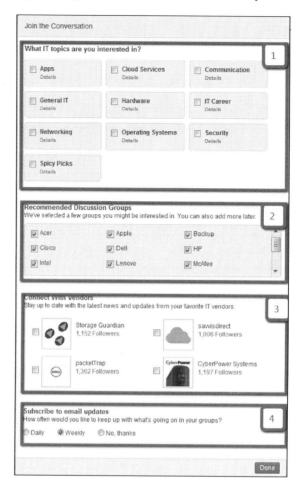

- The area highlighted as **1** shows the IT topic forums that you can be subscribed to. These are vendor specific, technology specific, or general IT topics.

- If you mouse over each IT discussion group in the area highlighted as **2**, you can see what forums each general topic consists of.

- Spiceworks suggests specific vendor pages in the area highlighted as **3**. Now, since there are over 1600+ vendor pages, there will be three or four on here but you can search for more later once you finish this step.

- The area highlighted as **4** is where you can opt for the Spiceworks newsletter. **Daily**, **Weekly**, and **No, thanks** options are here. Choose the one you want and then click on the **Done** button.

That's it! You are now a member of the most vibrant, answer-packed IT pro Community on the internet machine. Now we are going to come back to the Community a lot in this book. Since the Community is such a sprawling, awesome place, I suggest we get your network inventory and a few other things set up and then come back to it when you have some time to really explore.

Summary

Wow! Nice work so far! From not being sure as to what Spiceworks was to having a working install in just one chapter, fantastic. As we move through this book and you learn more and more about Spiceworks, you will realize how helpful Spiceworks is and how it can make your IT days easier. We cannot rest on our laurels, let's get to it and get some data in Spiceworks so that you can see how powerful it is! The next chapter consists of everything you need to know about network inventory. I know you want to get that going, so off we go.

2

Configuring Network Inventory in Spiceworks

As an IT pro, the more information you have about the devices on your network the better. The heart of the Spiceworks app is its network inventory, and it delivers a ton of information that you can use. One of the biggest challenges IT folks have is keeping up with changes on their network while supporting their users at the same time. Trying to manually go around and collect information is just not feasible; Spiceworks automates this process and dynamically updates this information for you. Sounds pretty awesome, doesn't it? Here is what we are going to cover:

- An overview of Spiceworks network scan

- Setting up a scan

- Navigating and customizing your Spiceworks inventory

- Group creation and scanning in Spiceworks

- Resolving unknown devices

As you go through this book and work with Spiceworks, you will realize the extent to which different parts of the app share information with each other. All of this starts with your network inventory. So let's jump right in and talk about what Spiceworks can scan.

An overview of the Spiceworks network inventory

Spiceworks can scan and collect information from most devices that have a network connection (and an OS). Windows, SSH, ESX/vSphere, and SNMP are all supported within Spiceworks among many others.

How Spiceworks scans your network

Here is the process of how Spiceworks scans devices on your network:

1. **Active Directory**: If Spiceworks has access to any local Active Directory domains (we will be going over this a little later in this chapter), it logs in and collects an inventory of assets on the network. Once the device is found, Spiceworks fills in specific fields based on the information collected. Some information that is collected is as follows:

   - IP address
   - Operating system
   - Service pack level
   - Machine name

2. **NetBIOS**: Spiceworks tries to access a machine's NetBIOS to collect any additional information it can.

3. **Scanning the IP address range**: Based on the scan settings that you set up (we will get to those in just a couple pages), Spiceworks scans a specific IP address range. In this scan, it sweeps the full range that has been defined and waits for a response. Spiceworks can also use Nmap to scan ranges under 256 addresses.

4. **Identification**: If a machine responds to Spiceworks, it is identified based on the port that Spiceworks can connect to.

5. **Collection**: Using protocols and credentials provided in the specific scan, the settings information for that device is collected.

6. **Classification**: Spiceworks categorizes the machine based on what information it can collect.

7. **The DNS report**: Spiceworks attempts to do both forward and reverse lookup in DNS and creates the report.

8. **Grouping**: Once the scan is finished, Spiceworks groups devices based on defaults or into custom groups that you can create.

9. **Logging**: During the scan, Spiceworks grabs any Windows events that you define.

As you can see, Spiceworks does a very good job at trying to identify any network-connected devices. The amount of information it also pulls from devices is really impressive. So how does Spiceworks pull this information once it connects to a device? Well, it has a list of ports that it tries on a device once it has responded to the IP range scan. You would ask, "What are these ports?" It is your lucky day as the list is right here:

- **Port 135 – WMI**: This is used for Windows devices.
- **Port 22 – SSH**: This is used for Unix/Linux/Mac/some network devices.
- **Port 16992 – Intel AMT HTTP/SOAP**: This is used for Intel vPro devices.
- **Port 9100 – HP Jet Direct**: This is used for printers.
- **Port 5060 – SIP**: This is used for IP phones.
- **Port 80 – HTTP**: This is used for servers. This is also used for VMware and NAS devices. Spiceworks also scans the web page for useful information to help classify the device into an inventory group. This helps with some switches, printers, or routers that have web pages.
- **Port 161 – SNMP**: This is used for network devices such as routers, switches, and some printers.
- **Port 5800 – VNC HTTP**: This is used to check if devices support VNC.

Now, a device on your network has to have a port open for Spiceworks to get into it and magically collect the wonderful information it does. If a device has a firewall in place or no ports are open, that is another matter. Spiceworks knows something is there, but just doesn't know what; so it classifies a device like that into the Unknown Devices group. We will be going over the best ways to resolve these later in the chapter. Let's just get to work on setting up a scan so you can see Spiceworks network inventory in action!

What else does Spiceworks scan?

We have gone over the process and ports that Spiceworks uses to scan devices on your network, but it also scans and retrieves other essential information from your network.

On every device that Spiceworks connects to, it not only reads hardware information, but also does a full software inventory and an OS hotfix history. This means in one scan itself you are getting full inventories in the following categories:

- **Hardware**: This includes details of motherboard, memory, processor, and disk configuration
- **Operating system**: This includes complete details on the operating system version

- **Hotfix/update history**: This includes a full list of hotfixes/updates that have been installed on the machine along with dates they were installed

- **Software**: This includes a list of all installed applications on every machine

- **Others**: This includes details on Mobile Device Management (MDM), Cloud services, and much more that can be administered through Spiceworks

If you are using Active Directory, Spiceworks logs in to your Domain Controller and reads your users, all your organizational units, and other information such as exchange servers and DNS data.

No doubt you have spent some time organizing your AD environment just the way you like it. Servers, workstations, users are all in specific OUs for Group Policy Management and other reasons. Well, Spiceworks can organize these devices and users in the same way so that they will be easy to find.

No need to reorganize everything on your network in Spiceworks! They do try and make it easy for us as IT pros.

Now that we have gone over Spiceworks scan process, ports, and what else it can scan, let's jump right into setting up our first scan!

Setting up a scan in Spiceworks

When we went over the Spiceworks device scan process at the beginning of this chapter, the first thing it tries to do is contact **Active Directory (AD)**; it also uses AD to populate the **People** portion of your Inventory. Let's set up AD first, as everything else we will be configuring is on the same page. We are all about saving your time and not going back and forth between pages.

If you do not have AD in your environment, you can just skip to the *Configuring IP range scans* section.

Scanning and Active Directory

There is a wealth of information within AD that Spiceworks uses. We are going to need to configure Spiceworks to log into AD and get that information.

OK, we need to get to the **Active Directory Configuration** screen in Spiceworks in order to do that. As with most things within the app, it is just a couple of clicks. From anywhere in the app, mouse over the **Inventory** link at the top of the page; a menu will open up. Click on **Settings**.

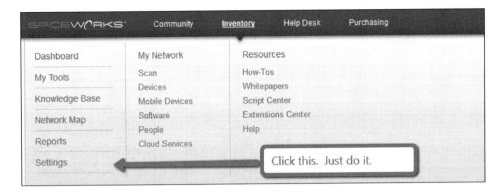

This will take us to the **Settings** screen. You will be spending a lot of time here in the coming chapters so you can either get very used to these clicks or just have a separate tab open with these settings already set up.

The top section is called **Getting Started** and the first link is **Active Directory Configuration**. That is our destination for this section so click away. It will take you to the **Active Directory Configuration** page:

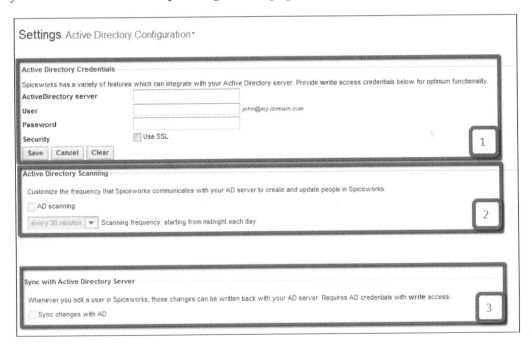

There are three sections that are highlighted. Let's go over each and what they do:

- The area highlighted as **1** is where you are going to enter the credentials that allow Spiceworks to log into your AD and get information. You specify the Active Directory Server (Domain Controller), username and password. Usernames must be in either domain/username or username@domain.com. If you have SSL enabled for AD inquiries, check the **Use SSL** box.

- The area highlighted as **2** shows the frequency at which Spiceworks retrieves information from your AD environment. When Spiceworks queries AD, it does not cause a huge amount of traffic or load. Shortening these times should not cause undue stress on your AD servers. This is useful because when you add a user in AD, it will automatically get loaded into Spiceworks at the next scan.

- If you want any changes you make to users in Spiceworks to be uploaded into your AD environment, the section highlighted as **3** is for you. Just click on the box and any modifications you make in Spiceworks will automatically be synchronized with your AD.

There is one more section that is not in the screenshot. This deals with your user portal and help desk. We will be going over this in *Chapter 3, Configuring the Spiceworks Help Desk and User Portal,* so don't worry about it right now.

Setting up AD in your Spiceworks really makes a lot of difference with scans and filling in information. It is recommended that if you are running AD, hook this up. If you are wary about Spiceworks writing data into your AD environment, just set up the user that Spiceworks uses to connect as read-only and don't check the box that writes changes back to AD. Easy enough.

Since you are convinced that you should connect your AD to Spiceworks, just fill in the **ActiveDirectory server**, **User**, and **Password** fields and click on **Save**. Spiceworks will automatically test the credentials and let you know immediately if it can connect.

If you have some challenges with Spiceworks connecting to your Domain Controller with just the server name, another method is to put the IP address directly into that field.

Let's move on to setting up an IP range scan and get some devices into your Spiceworks install.

Configuring IP range scans

Remember the **Settings** page that we have been to a couple of times? We are going back! In case you have forgotten, just mouse over to either **Inventory** or **Help Desk** and click on the **Settings** link at the bottom of the left column.

Once on the **Settings** page, we are going to click on the **Network Scan** link. It is in the first section of links titled **Getting Started**. This takes us to the main **Network Scan** page. The first section is where we are going to set up our IP ranges.

Since you will not have any ranges in here as you just installed Spiceworks, let's get one configured so you can get some information into the app. To do this, just click on the **Add IP Range** button and this window will pop up.

There is a lot of flexibility that Spiceworks gives you regarding how it scans IP ranges. You can put a fill range (`192.168.1.1-254`) with or without exclusions, or just a single IP if you so wish. The next box is for exclusions, if you so choose. If you decide you want to scan a range that has both servers and desktops, you can exclude server IP addresses. This is handy.

The last options are for scheduling this IP range scan. If you choose the **Daily at...** option as we have seen in the screenshot, you can also select the time of the day to run this scan. Other options in this drop-down list are every 4, 6, 8, or 12 hours. If you do decide that you want to scan on an hourly basis, the time of the day magically disappears. The bottom of the window lets you select what days of the week you want to run the scan.

When Spiceworks runs an initial scan, it can take a bit of time as there is a ton of data that it is collecting. Spiceworks tries a multitude of credentials and reads all information from devices, which it then writes to the database. Once Spiceworks has scanned and written the data to the database, any subsequent scans just write delta data into it.

Enter what range you want to scan, any exclusions you choose, and the scan frequency, and click on the **Add** button.

Congratulations! You have just added an IP range scan!

Scanning credentials

As we have covered, Spiceworks uses a multitude of credentials to try and figure out what is on your network and put those devices into the inventory. The next section on the **Network Scan** page is where you can input all those credentials.

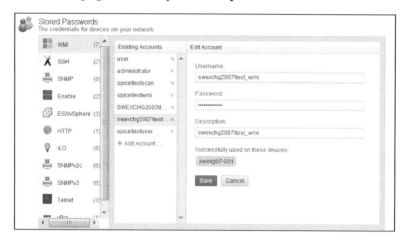

This has been completely overhauled in Spiceworks. In this easy-to-use interface, you can enter all the credentials that you are going to need to have a successful scan. Here you can configure multiple usernames/passwords for the following protocols:

- **WMI**
- **SSH**
- **SNMP**
- **Enable**
- **ESX/vSphere**
- **HTTP**
- **iLo**
- **SNMP v2c/v3**
- **Telnet**
- **Intel vPro**

As you can see, if you need to put device-specific usernames and passwords into Spiceworks, you can do so using the format, Domain\username.

So if you have a server that uses a unique username/password combination, it is easy to set all that up through this interface. The preceding screenshot shows an example of this. Something new in Spiceworks is the section where it shows devices that the credentials were successfully used on. This is really helpful for troubleshooting any scan errors!

To add your own username/password combinations, just use these easy-to-follow directions:

1. Click on the protocol you want to add credentials to on the left column (**WMI**, **SNMP**, and so on).

2. Click on **+Add Account** in the middle column labeled **Existing Accounts**.

3. Enter all the pertinent information on the left pane labeled **Edit Account**. For usernames that have passwords, there is a **Show Password** button as well, so you can make sure that you didn't fat finger it!

That's it. Just fill in any credentials that will let Spiceworks access your devices on your network, and as far as permissions are concerned you should be good to go!

Best practices and kicking off your first Spiceworks scan

You have everything you need to start your first Spiceworks scan. It might be best to read the following best practices before you kick it off, though. They will guide you through some potential pitfalls.

Scanning best practices

For initial scans, be aware of the number of IP addresses you are scanning and the amount of information that Spiceworks is going to pull out of those devices.

- If you put in a full IP range on your first scan, do not expect Spiceworks to be completed in 10-15 minutes. The initial scan is the most network traffic intensive and will take the longest duration of time.

- Do full initial scans during nonbusiness hours. Though running an initial full scan shouldn't flood your network, depending on your network configuration, it is always best to run full initial scans during nonbusiness hours just in case. If you are running a 24 x 7 business, break up your IP ranges into smaller chunks and scan that way.

- Expect some unknown devices. Unless you are a super administrator with a team of hundreds behind you to make sure that every aspect of your network is 100 percent buttoned down, there will most likely be a few devices that Spiceworks cannot connect to. One of the biggest culprits is that WMI has been disabled, or that there is a firewall of some sort blocking Spiceworks from connecting to the machine. Don't get down on yourself if the scan doesn't work 100 percent the first time.

- If you are really worried about traffic that Spiceworks might cause, what information it collects, or how it will affect workstation performance, just set up a test environment and run a scan there. Whether it be 5 machines or 500, Spiceworks does the same to each one; so test away.

- Spiceworks is not designed to scan 10,000 devices at one time without a performance hit. If you have a very large network, break it up into smaller chunks for best performance. Spiceworks could get through a 10,000 device scan, but it would hurt performance until the scan is complete.

- If you have multiple sites linked either by WAN or VPN connections, drop a remote collector at these to run local scans and then send the data back to your main Spiceworks installation. You can find more information at `http://community.spiceworks.com/help/Remote_Collectors`.

OK, now that you have read the required best practices, you can set up your IP range on the **Network Scan** settings page, check the box associated with that range and click on **Start Scan**. Away you go!

Depending on the IP range you set and the time of the day, your scan could take just a few minutes or several hours.

If you are having some serious issues trying to get a successful scan, open a browser and hit this site: `http://community.spiceworks.com/support`.

There are in-depth articles and even real-live support folks that can dive into the specifics of your environment, and they won't give up until you are successful.

Let's assume that even if you did have an issue, it is resolved and you have got your first scan under your belt. Fantastic! Let's dive right into navigating the inventory itself.

Navigating the Spiceworks inventory

Now, having inventory in Spiceworks is no good unless we can access it. We are going to go through navigating the different parts of Spiceworks inventory, what you can and cannot do, and even a few tricks on how to customize it for your own requirements

As mentioned earlier in this chapter, Spiceworks gleans a ton of information from devices it scans; not only hardware, but also software and even users on your network. Spiceworks has interfaces for each category of these out of the box. Let's show you how to access them.

Navigating the device inventory

Once your scan has completed, just mouse over the **Inventory** tab at the top of any page in the app and you will see a link to **Devices** in the **My Network** column. Just click on that and the following screen will appear:

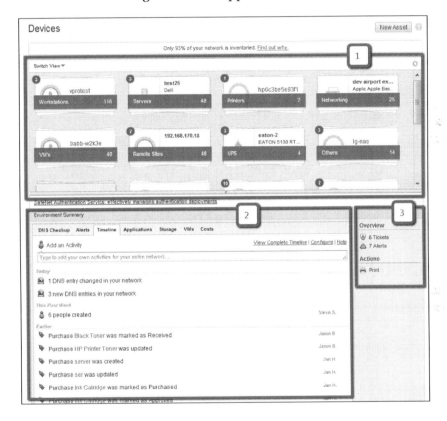

Spiceworks should have already automatically categorized many of your devices. This screen is the gateway to administering all that glorious information. Let's go through the main sections:

- Here is the icon view of your inventory that is highlighted as **1**. Devices have been automatically sorted into these groups. Just click on any group and you will be taken to a page where instead of a group view like we have, it will be populated with the machines in that individual group.

- This is the information pane that is highlighted as **2**. Where we are, at the top level, there are a set of tabs that you can click on to get different information on your network as a whole. These tabs are:
    - **DNS Checkup**: If any devices failed either a forward or reverse lookup during the scan or any devices that cannot be resolved in DNS, the results are shown here.
    - **Alerts**: If you set up any alerts (we will go over that in *Chapter 4, Configuring Other Spiceworks Features*), and if they are triggered, you will see the results here.
    - **Timeline**: This tracks anything that happens in Spiceworks. Tickets, devices, people or purchases being created, DNS entries changing, or any other change, an entry shows up here when it happens.
    - **Applications**: A list of the 100 most recently installed applications across your entire network, along with the computer name and date installed.
    - **Storage**: This shows how much free space is on any computer that Spiceworks has scanned along with the drive name, size, and percentage of free space.
    - **VMs**: If you have virtual hosts on your network and have given credentials to log in to those for your scan, individual virtual machines will show up here. You can even expand these virtual machines and turn on/off right through this interface.
    - **Costs**: If you configure purchasing through Spiceworks, you can track costs through this interface. We will be going through purchasing in *Chapter 4, Configuring Other Spiceworks Features*.

- **Overview**: Here you can see any help desk tickets that are open, any alerts that have been triggered, and also the ability to print any tab you are currently on.

With just a couple of clicks, you can get such good information on your network. One more thing regarding this page. We mentioned that this is the icon view of your inventory. There is another view that can be very helpful in finding information easily. If you mouse over the **Switch View** dropdown at the top of the icon pane, there is another option called **Browse View**. Here is an example of that view:

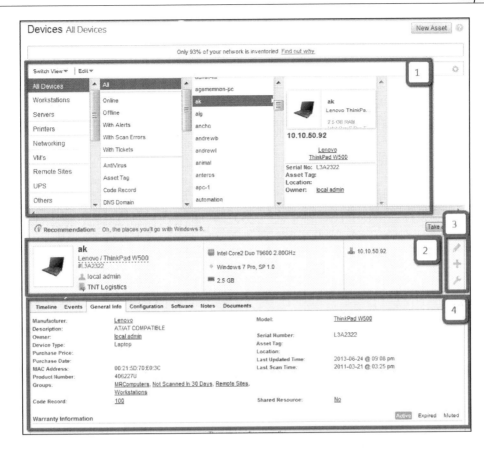

Notice the difference between this view and the one before. Let's go through some of the highlighted areas:

- Instead of icons, there is a list that you can drill down into in the area highlighted as **1**. The groups that were in the icon view are on the far left; the next column has a multitude of different attributes that you can sort by. The next column shows devices that are in the group to the left and finally you see an overview of the machine that you select. This overview includes the device name, IP address, make and model of device along with serial number, asset tag, location, and owner.

- The area highlighted as **2** is where we see a more detailed pane for the same device as the pane above it. This pane is dynamic in that whatever device you click on in **Browse View**, the details will be presented here. You have some more detailed information such as processor, OS, amount of memory, primary group, and IP address.

- You will be using the icons in the area highlighted as **3** a lot. Mouse over them and notice the submenus that show up.
    - The top icon (pencil) is what you click to edit any attribute on this device.
    - The middle icon (the + sign) is where you can add a ticket, purchase, or warranty to this device.
    - The bottom icon (wrench) opens an expansive menu of tools—which includes Ping, Traceroute, Remote Control, nslookup, and many more—that you can use directly on this device. You can also see running processes using this icon. This icon is very, very useful.

- The area highlighted as **4** is a pane similar to the one we see when we are looking at our whole network. Here is a quick overview of these tabs:
    - **Timeline**: This tab provides a timeline of changes to this specific machine
    - **Events**: This tab shows the Windows event log
    - **General Info**: This tab shows expanded information about the machine itself
    - **Configuration**: This tab shows specific information about hardware, software, and even active network connections
    - **Software**: This tab shows all installed software on the machine
    - **Notes**: This tab shows any notes that have been taken for this machine
    - **Documents**: This tab shows any documents that have been uploaded into Spiceworks about this machine

 You can get the same information through the icon view of your inventory as well. You just have to double-click on a group and then on a specific machine.

Now you should be getting a feel for how powerful Spiceworks can be! Having all this information in one interface can be a lifesaver for a busy IT pro. Play around the inventory interface. Some folks like icons, some folks like browsing. Totally a matter of preference, as you can get the same information either way.

Remember, this is only the device inventory. Let's briefly go over the other inventories.

Navigating other inventories

If you mouse over the **Inventory** link at the top of any page in the app, you will see not only **Devices**, but other inventories as well.

- **Devices**: We have gone over this in the previous section.

- **Mobile Devices**: We will go over this briefly in *Chapter 4, Configuring Other Spiceworks Features*.

- **Software**: This is a robust inventory of all software installed across your entire network.

- **People**: Spiceworks reads Active Directory, extracts information from user objects, and populates users in this inventory.

- **Cloud Services**: You can configure Spiceworks to log in to and monitor many Cloud services, which we will briefly go over in *Chapter 4, Configuring Other Spiceworks Features*.

The Software inventory

Clicking on the **Software** link when you mouse over Inventory in Spiceworks brings you to **Dashboard**. This is a useful interface and we can set up some alerts, which we will touch on in *Chapter 4, Configuring Other Spiceworks Features*, but we want to really be able to dig into our data, right? Have a look at the following screenshot:

In this screenshot, we can see the different software inventory interfaces. Let's go through them briefly:

- **Applications**: This gives us every application that is installed on every machine on our network. On larger networks, this list can be very long. It also includes earliest and latest versions and number of installs. When clicking on a specific application, it will display what machines have that specific app installed and even the date it was installed on. A fantastic way for you to get a high-level view of software installs on your network.

- **Licensed**: This view is basically a subset of the Applications view, in that it only includes software that specifically needs a license. All the same functionality as the Applications view.

- **Unwanted**: Here is software that you can classify as unwanted. Spiceworks will also alert you if any new installs show up on scans.

- **Services**: When Spiceworks scans, it automatically reads any services that are running on a device. Here is where you can search for any and all services that might be running on your network. As with the previous entries, this view will tell you which computers have a specific service running, but in addition it will tell you how many of those computers have it stopped or started.

- **Hotfixes**: These are any and all hotfixes for Windows computers that are installed on your network. As with the rest of this list, it will tell you which computers have it installed, which ones do not, and dates of installation.

This is a fantastic tool for an IT pro. From volume licensing compliance, monitoring rogue installs of bad software to knowing who has what toolbar installed on their browser, being able to get this information in such an easy manner will make your day so much easier.

The People inventory

When you mouse over **Inventory** at the top of any page in the app (tired of hearing us say that yet?) and then click on **People**, it will take you to the **People Inventory** interface.

These are strictly set up based on your AD structure. Have a look at some of your users and look at the information that Spiceworks brought over. Names, locations, e-mail addresses, phone numbers, supervisors, and much more are here.

This really gives us the ability to associate devices, help desk tickets, and purchases with real users within our environment. So, you will be able to retrieve information from a multitude of sources, which saves a boatload of time.

Whew! We just went through a whirlwind of views, dashboards, and a ton of information in a very short period of time. A good suggestion would be to play with the different views in each category and find the one that works best for you. There is no wrong way to get what information you need in Spiceworks!

Alright, so now that you are an expert in how Spiceworks scans a network, a guru in setting up IP range scans, and a professional in navigating the different inventories, the next step on your road to your Spiceworks dominance is to go into how to customize different scans and set up some groups. No rest for you, let's get right to it.

Customizing groups and scan schedules

We briefly went over the Spiceworks scan process at the beginning of this chapter; once Spiceworks scans, it automatically classifies devices into groups. We saw that in the *Navigating the device inventory* section. Here is exactly how Spiceworks groups those devices:

- **Desktops**: These are machines that respond to WMI or SSH ports, do not have a battery installed, and are not running a server OS.

- **Laptops**: These are machines that respond to WMI or SSH ports and have a battery installed.

- **Servers**: These are machines that respond to WMI, SSH, or HTTP ports and are running a server OS such as Linux, Windows Server, or VMware.

- **Network devices**: These are machines that respond to SNMP or SSH.

- **Network printers**: These are printers that respond to HTTP, Jet Direct, or SNMP.

- **VOIP**: This is a machine that responds to the SIP port.

- **UPS**: This is determined by SNMP, WMI, or SSH queries.

- **Virtual devices**: These are defined by HTTP queries to virtual hosts.

- **Unknowns**: These are machines that are not defined by AD and do not have any open ports.

A device that is scanned by Spiceworks can and probably will be in multiple groups between AD groups and the preceding ones. So, what if you need a group that isn't in Active Directory and not in the preceding list? Simple, you create a custom group! Custom groups, you may ask? Absolutely! The process to create these is a pretty simple one. Let's go through it.

1. Navigate to the **Settings** page, you should know how to do that by now.

2. Under **Additional Settings**, there is a link for **Custom Groups**, click on it.

3. You will find yourself on the **Custom Groups** screen. Here you can see all the current groups. There will be some from your AD structure and ones that Spiceworks has automatically put devices in.

4. There is a button at the bottom-left area of the window that contains the current groups called **New Group**, click on that to open the new group options below.

At this point, it would probably be easier to explain this with a screenshot. As it happens, there is a screenshot right here:

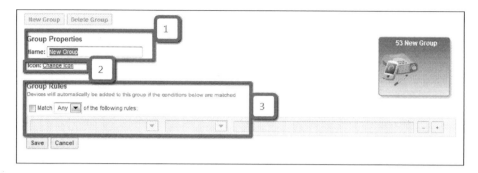

This menu looks pretty simple, and on the surface it is. But beware, it can get pretty complex quickly. Lets' look at the highlighted areas:

- The area highlighted as **1** is where you are going to enter the name of the new group.

- Click on the **Change Icon** link in the area highlighted as **2** to change the icon for the group.

- The area highlighted as **3** is the rule portion of the group. Spiceworks can create both manual and dynamic groups. If you want to put people/devices into this group by hand, just keep this box unchecked. The group will be visible and you can put whatever you want in it. Honestly though, we are IT folks, we love to automate things. I think a rule-based dynamic group is for you. If you want to go down that road, just check the box and create the conditions for devices to be automatically put in this group.

From this simple interface you can really create some awesome, dynamic groups for things such as groups of desktops that have their antivirus definitions expired, machines with less than a certain amount of memory, and a certain processor. The possibilities are endless and instead of searching around for information, you can just look in for one of your custom groups to find all machines that fit the criteria! Brilliant!

Now, there are several reasons for carving out custom groups. Some I mentioned in the previous paragraph and here is a big one.

Spiceworks can schedule some unique group-specific scans. They are:

- **All**: This is a complete inventory of devices including software, configuration, hardware, resources, and events.

- **Resources**: This queries capabilities for disks, network adapters, mailboxes, and so on.

- **Utilization**: This shows system and network utilization.

- **Events**: This shows Windows events.

- **Up/Down**: Pings devices in the group to confirm network connection.

That's right, you can schedule custom and default group scans with the preceding criteria. Let's go into how that is exactly accomplished:

1. Let's hit the **Settings** screen and then click on the **Network Scan** link; we have been there before earlier in this chapter.

2. Scroll down until you see the **Schedules** portion of the page; here is where we are going to set up your new custom scan.

3. To the right of the **Schedules** title, there is an **Add Schedule** button. Click on it.

A window will pop up with a bunch of fields that you have to fill in to set up your scheduled scan. We could try and struggle through each one with words, but a screenshot is worth a thousand of those:

Looking at this, the **Scan Type** drop-down list lets you choose what kind of custom scan you want to run. We went over these on the last page. The next field is dynamic. Just start typing the name of whatever group you want to scan and a list will pop up allowing you to choose the one you want. Next, choose the time and days you want to run the scan. Lastly, there is a checkbox to disable the scan schedule.

This is a really powerful toolset for you to monitor a specific group of machines and it is brand new in Spiceworks. Set up a couple of schedules and have fun.

Resolving unknown devices

Even if you are a super IT pro, when you do an initial scan with Spiceworks, you are probably going to have some unknown devices. Well, if you have a very small network of five machines, perhaps not. Anyway, Spiceworks has a tool that will help you with resolving these unknowns.

Direct your mouse over the **Inventory** link at the top of any page in the app and instead of clicking on **Settings**, like you are used to by this point, you are going to click on the **Scan** link under **My Network**. The **Scan Overview** page will appear, as if by magic. This is a brand spanking new page in Spiceworks and it has a ton of information on it. Let's go through some of the important areas:

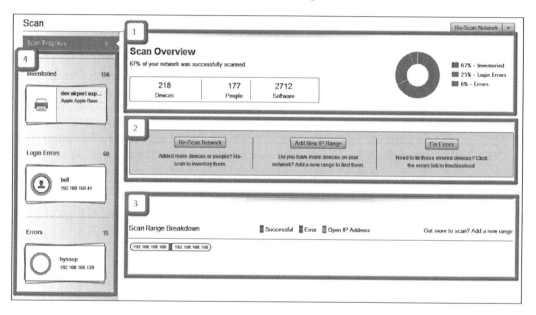

We have broken it up into four major areas:

- The area highlighted as **1** is the **Scan Overview** pane. At a glance, it will tell you exactly how many devices, how many people, and the number of different pieces of software on your network. The pie chart on the right-hand side also tells you by percentage what has been inventoried and what hasn't by login errors and other errors.

- The area highlighted as **2** is what is commonly called the action pane on your **Scan** page. Here, you can kick off a scan that you have already set up by clicking on the **Re-Scan Network** button, add a new IP range by clicking on the **Add New IP Range** button, or open the new interface to resolve unknown devices by clicking on the **Fix Errors** button.

- The area highlighted as **3** is an overview of scans you currently have set up and if there were any errors within those ranges.

- The area highlighted as **4** is another overview pane but instead of a pie chart like we see on the **Scan Overview** pane, here we can see the exact number of inventoried devices, the ones with login errors, and the ones with other errors. Another difference is that you can click on both **Login Errors** and **Errors** to launch a tool to help you fix those errors.

Some great information is here for you. As Spiceworks further develops these tools, there will be even more added functionality. What we are specifically looking for right now is the pane on the left. It is the area highlighted as **4** in the preceding screenshot. If you have errors causing devices to be classified as unknown devices, this is a great way to figure those out. If you click on **Login Errors**, you will find yourself on a screen similar to the following:

Now this is what we are talking about when we need to find specifics on why Spiceworks cannot connect to a device. It even has a **Degree of Difficulty** gauge. If you click on the **Fix Errors** button under either of the **Type of Error** numbers, a screen like the following one comes up. Here, you will find all the devices that Spiceworks couldn't log into with the provided credentials.

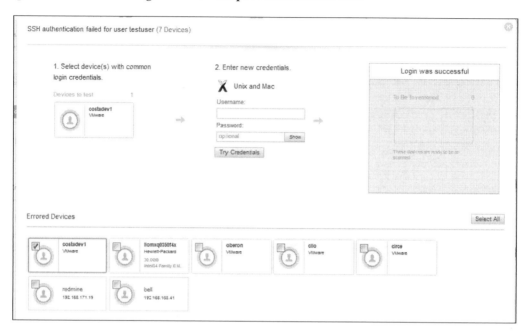

Do you need a tool to figure out what credentials work? This is the tool for you! You can select devices that have failed from the bottom pane and they will automatically move to the top-right pane. Then, just put in the credentials that you think are going to work and click on the **Try Connection** button. Spiceworks will try those credentials and let you know if they are good.

This is really helpful for resolving those login errors. One last screenshot from the regular **Errors** screen instead of **Login Errors** is as follows:

If you notice, on the **Login Errors** page, the **Degree of Difficulty** gauges were all in the green area. Here they are all orange or red. In addition, this menu tells you exactly what errors exist with what machines. Spiceworks has really made it easy for you to either fix or remove problematic devices.

Summary

Well, you probably entered this chapter not knowing what kind of power Spiceworks had under its hood. By now, you ought to have a pretty good idea and we are not even halfway through the book! You have some devices in your inventory, some software as well as people, and a good idea of how to resolve any errors that were encountered in your initial scan.

This is a lot of information to take in and you are just doing outstanding. The next chapter is all help desk and user portal, so you can play around with your new inventory toys or jump right into it. On we go on our Spiceworks journey!

3

Configuring the Spiceworks Help Desk and User Portal

Whether you are a solo IT Professional or a team of 40, having an efficient help desk is the cornerstone for any IT department. A help desk is more than just a ticketing system; it is a way for you to track internal resources, track the time spent in resolving an issue, and even prioritizing the current open issues.

One of the huge advantages of Spiceworks over other products in the help desk space is its tight integration between different parts of the application. Information in one facet of the application is accessible in many other facets. So in a single pane of glass, you have all the information you need at a glance. The help desk is no exception to this rule. Tickets can be opened to track purchases associated to users and computers or devices, and rules could be put in place to automate many common tasks. Let's have an overview of what we are going to cover in this chapter:

- An overview of the Help Desk interface and the User Portal
- Setting up users, permissions, and the e-mail functionality
- Configuring User Portal
- Using custom attributes
- Creating tickets
- Ways of working the tickets in Spiceworks
- Extending the User Portal and Help Desk with plugins

Yup, you did read that right; we are going to cover all these topics. I highly suggest you grab your energizing beverage of choice as this is going to be a wild ride. Let's get right to it!

An overview of the Help Desk interface and User Portal

There are two interfaces of the Spiceworks' Help Desk as follows:

- The first is for admins and IT staff, and we will be calling it the **Administrative Interface (AI)**.

- The second is for the users you will provide support to open tickets, modify or check the status of open tickets, and get IT information. This is called the **User Portal (UP)**.

If you have used any kind of commercial Help Desk application, these concepts should be pretty familiar to you. If they are not, don't despair, we will be getting very friendly with each of them.

To get to the AI from anywhere in Spiceworks, click on the **Help Desk** link at the top of the page. Once you open **Help Desk**, you will see a page as shown in the following screenshot:

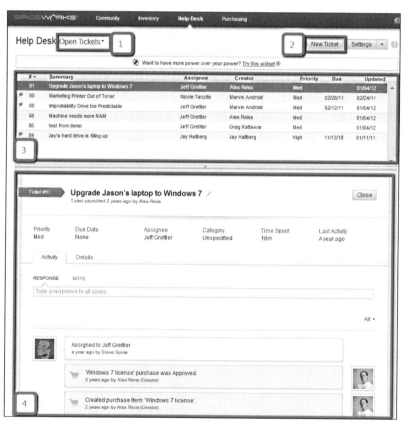

Let's go through the main parts of the AI; the explanation for highlighted areas in the preceding screenshot are as follows:

- The area highlighted as **1** is actually a plugin that comes along with the installation of Spiceworks and is called My Ticket Views. This plugin provides a quick access menu to define which Help Desk tickets will be displayed. It is a fully customizable way to create different views on your tickets and keep your Help Desk running like a boss.

- If you need to create a new ticket, just click on the **New Ticket** button The area highlighted as **2**. We will be going over the process to allow users to open tickets themselves (the preferred way for the users to let you know that their keyboard is unplugged or anything else they may be having an issue with). There will be times though where you will want to create a ticket yourself, and to do that, click on the **New Ticket** button.

- The area highlighted as **3** is the Ticket Summary section. You can see at a glance the ticket number, summary, creator, priority, the due date (if applicable), and the date the ticket was last updated. This is a great way to browse tickets.

- The area highlighted as **4** is the Ticket Details pane. When you click on a ticket in the Ticket Summary section, this information dynamically changes to fill in any ticket details. You will do most of the editing of tickets in this section of the Help Desk.

There you have it, the Help Desk AI in a nutshell. Pretty intuitive, isn't it? We will be getting into more of the nitty-gritty of working a ticket a little later in this chapter; we just wanted to get ourselves familiar with the interface.

Next, we need to create some user accounts in here so the IT Support staff can actually do some work.

Setting up Spiceworks users, permissions, and e-mail

We went over the different user levels in *Chapter 1, Setting Up Spiceworks*, but in case you didn't read that section, here is a brief overview:

- **Admin**: These users have full administrative privileges within Spiceworks.

- **Help Desk Admin**: These users have full administrative access to the Help Desk section of Spiceworks.

- **Help Desk Tech**: These users only have access to the Help Desk tickets that they are either assigned or copied on.

- **Reporting**: These users only have access to the reporting portion of Spiceworks.

 Now if you are a solo IT Professional in an office, you won't have to worry about adding additional users. You can just skip ahead to setting up the e-mail account and templates. You can't assume we aren't looking out for solo IT Professionals out there.

As we had discussed in *Chapter 1, Setting Up Spiceworks*, if you are wondering whether you would have to configure accounts for every end user (non-IT folks) who is going to use the Help Desk User Portal, don't worry, you won't have to do that. As users log into the User Portal, a user account will automatically be created for them, and no IT pro action is needed.

You already set up your main Admin users after you installed Spiceworks, so now we have to set up your Help Desk staff so they can view and work on tickets. This process is really straightforward and similar to creating Admin users within Spiceworks. Here are the steps:

1. To navigate to this page of Spiceworks, just move your cursor over the **Help Desk** link at the top of the page, and click on **Settings** on the right-hand side.

2. Once you are on the **Settings** page, click on the **User Accounts** link in the **Personal** section.

3. Adding users for a Help Desk role is the same as adding a Spiceworks Admin, except in the **Access** column where you click on the dropdown and select either help desk **Admin** or **Tech**.

4. Click on **Save** to commit changes into Spiceworks.

5. The last step is to configure what e-mail is received by these folks. Fortunately, Spiceworks has the **Help Desk** option, which means they won't get alerts or weekly reports but just e-mails from Spiceworks regarding the Help Desk. Click on that option in the **Email Notifications** column for each of the users you just created and you are good to go.

We are talking a lot about e-mail, so the next step is to configure the e-mail settings in Spiceworks.

Configuring the e-mail settings in Spiceworks

Spiceworks uses e-mails not only for sending out notifications to the IT staff, but also for sending out updates on tickets to end users and sending out scheduled reports. Spiceworks even monitors a mailbox and creates tickets based on messages that get sent to that mailbox. Yes, you read that right. You can configure Spiceworks to monitor a specific mailbox, and it will automatically create a ticket for any message that is received by the inbox. So if you have a mailbox that your users send their issues to (or if you don't, I would highly suggest creating one), migrating to Spiceworks Help Desk is going to be a breeze! The last part of this section will be an overview of e-mail templates, and how you can exactly customize what you send through an e-mail.

Let's head back to the Help Desk AI to set up all of these. Click on the **Help Desk** link on the top of the page, and look right next to the **New Ticket** button for **Settings**. Click the drop-down arrow to expand this menu to include both the **Help Desk** and **Email Setup** options. You can refer to the following screenshot:

This is going to open up the **Email Settings** wizard. One of the reasons we came here instead of staying on the **Settings** page is because Spiceworks bundles most e-mail settings into this single wizard so we can set up everything in one go. Spiceworks has numbered these steps, but since we are rebels, we won't be following their suggestions to the letter (as we will be going through the User Portal in the next section of this chapter). We are going to skip the first option and jump directly to the second one, **Configuring Spiceworks to Send and Receive Email**. A menu slides into place that has everything we need to get this step completed.

Before we jump into setting up the e-mail account, there are a few things that you should be careful about. At this stage of your Spiceworks configuration, Spiceworks does not know the difference between junk e-mails and valid requests. This includes out-of-office replies. The e-mail address that you configure here should serve only one purpose, that is, of being a help desk e-mail address, and should not be on any e-mail the distribution lists. Failing to do so might cause a feedback loop.

For example, If an e-mail arrives in the Help Desk inbox from a distribution list where the Help Desk is a member, Spiceworks creates a ticket and sends a confirmation e-mail back to the originator. In this case that is a distribution list that has the Help Desk e-mail on it. That e-mail arrives in the Help Desk inbox and Spiceworks automatically updates the ticket and sends out a confirmation back to the distribution list. This causes an endless loop where Spiceworks itself is creating updates to a single ticket. IT Professionals who come to the office and open Spiceworks find that they have received hundreds of e-mails due to this. Needless to say, it wasn't a good morning for them! So just make sure that the mailbox you set up in this section is solely for Help Desk requests. We will be going through ticket rules at the end of this chapter, so don't worry, we have your back.

Now let's get back to the task at hand. The menu we opened comprises three sections:

- **Display Information**: This section deals with the name and e-mail address that will be present in the **From** field of the outgoing e-mails. An important thing to remember in this section is what you fill into the e-mail address field is the reply-to address. I highly suggest putting in the Spiceworks-monitored e-mail box that we will configure in Step 3 in the **Sender Email** field, or else you will lose most of the functionality the Help Desk provides.

- **Outgoing Email**: This section deals with the Outgoing Email server. This can be either a local exchange e-mail server or any SMTP e-mail server. This includes cloud-based e-mail services, so you don't need a local SMTP server for e-mail to be sent out. Note that this server should be the same e-mail system (either cloud or local) as your monitored mailbox. Although you don't have to do it in this way, there is a very high chance that spam filters will classify any Spiceworks e-mail as spam if the outgoing mail server is not the MX record for the domain that is in the reply-to address.

- **Incoming Email**: This is one of the most important settings in the Spiceworks Help Desk. As we went through right before jumping into this menu, Spiceworks can monitor a mailbox, create tickets, and update existing tickets based on messages that arrive in it. Both IT Professionals and end users can update the tickets via e-mail. IMAP, Exchange, and POP are all supported here. Fill in the details for either your cloud or local mailbox.

Let's dig deeper into the **Incoming Mail** setting and what it means to you. This is a very powerful feature and one that comes out of the box in your Spiceworks installation. If anyone sends a message to the mailbox specified in the **Incoming Mail** field, depending on the subject line, Spiceworks creates a ticket extracting information from the e-mail. The **Email Sender** becomes **Ticket Creator**, **Email Subject** becomes **Ticket Summary**, **Email Body** becomes **Ticket Description**. Once Spiceworks creates a ticket, it then sends an e-mail to both the creator (sender of the e-mail) and also any Spiceworks users who have Help Desk e-mail notifications enabled.

We are done with this wizard. Just click on **Save** to close the screen, and then click on **Done** to close the wizard. We have set up a mailbox for Spiceworks to monitor as well as configure a **From** e-mail address and the name of the sender. Now it is time to specify who receives these e-mails.

To get to the Help Desk settings page, just click on the **Settings** button (the same menu we dropped down to get to the **Email Setup** wizard). This takes us right to the Help Desk settings page. There is a lot going on here, so let's go through the different sections at a higher level:

- **Admin Email Notifications**: This section allows you to specify in some detail about who receives the e-mails when different actions take place in the lifecycle of a help desk ticket, and it has three columns:
    - **All**: Full admins and Help Desk admins within Spiceworks
    - **Assignee**: The Help Desk Tech role that receives e-mails when a ticket is assigned to them.
    - **Copied Admin or Tech**: Any admins or Help Desk Techs who are copied on the ticket

- **User Email Notifications**: This section provides details about end user communication the same way the above section does. This can be fantastic to keep your users updated on open tickets. There are two columns here:
    - **Submitter**: This column specifies whether the originator of the ticket is e-mailed when changes to the ticket are done.
    - **Copied Users**: This column specifies whether any users in the "Cc" field within a Help Desk ticket are e-mailed when changes to the ticket are done

- **Ticket Notification Templates**: This section allows you to modify the ticket template notifications. The template out of the box is pretty robust, so you shouldn't have to modify anything at this time. Make a note of where this section is located though as you may want to modify these notifications in the future.

- **Help Desk Extensions**: In this section, you should see both **My Ticket Rules** and **My Ticket Views** as checked. These are plugins that are installed out of the box with Spiceworks. There should be a third plugin here as well, although not checked, named **LogMeIn Rescue**. If you use this product to connect to remote workstations, this would be your lucky day as it is fully integrated with Spiceworks.

- **Labor Cost**: Here is where you can put the value of time for Help Desk technicians. Filling in this information is great not only for Managed Services Providers, but also for creating reports detailing work done in real dollars.

- **Optional Functionality**: Check the boxes next to the features you want to implement. Some of these include automatically assigning a Help Desk Ticket to any Admin that comment on it through the Spiceworks Desktop, allowing tickets to be deleted and enabling HTTPS on the User Portal.

- **Bulk Ticket Delete**: This section is useful if you find that someone spammed the mailbox Spiceworks was monitoring, and it then created many tickets based on those spam e-mails.

- **Ticket Import**: This section is for importing tickets from other Help Desk ticketing solutions.

That's it for e-mail settings! Don't worry if you didn't have all the information that you needed to fill all of this in as you read; these can easily be changed at any time.

The next section of the chapter involves the **Active Directory (AD)** integration within Spiceworks; if you do not use AD, you can just skip to the *Configuring User Portal* section.

The last step in this section of the chapter is to integrate Active Directory into our Help Desk. This way, users can log in to our User Portal and open their own tickets with their AD credentials (along with some other cool stuff that you can do). We have been there before setting up AD for our Network Inventory. Just move the cursor over the **Inventory** or **Help Desk** links at the top of any page in the app and click on **Settings**. Then click on the **Active Directory Configuration** link. This takes you to the page devoted to AD.

You should have already configured most of these fields when we were setting up our first network scan. What we are looking for here is the Portal Integration section. You might have to scroll down as depending on your screen resolution, it may not be initially visible on your screen. Checking this box just lets users use their AD username and password on our User Portal when they create their own tickets. One less password for them to remember. Brilliant!

We have talked a lot about users creating their own tickets within Spiceworks through the User Portal; let's configure that functionality right now.

Configuring User Portal

Out of the box, Spiceworks provides a customizable User Portal. We have focused on an end user's ability to open their own tickets and check on the status of those tickets up to this point, but the User Portal can provide much more than that. You can create different tabs on the portal or create widgets that can provide information to the end users, network status updates, and even the weather among many more. The tools for creating this content are also included in every Spiceworks installation.

There are two tools that Spiceworks provides in order to publish the User Portal:

- **Portal Designer**: This tool helps you design and test the look and feel of your portal. You can add or remove articles, pages, and knowledge-base entries along with changing logos.
- **Content Manager**: This tool allows you to create articles, pages, and knowledge-base entries.

The User Portal is a fantastic tool. It can simplify your Help Desk procedures and really make your users feel empowered (not to mention the e-mail and phone traffic into the Help Desk will go down drastically). Now let's find out how you can implement all of these wonderful features into your Spiceworks installation.

Just move your cursor over **Help Desk** at the top of the page, and click on the **User Portal** link on the right-hand side. This takes us to the page where we can get to both the Portal Designer and Content Manager tools. Currently, there isn't any content to design, so let's create a basic article. Click on **Content Manager** and it opens up. The following is an overview on the different sections of this page:

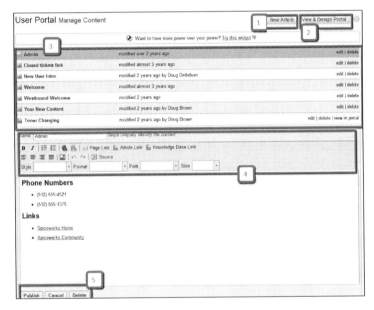

The following explains the highlighted portions in the preceding screenshot:

- The area highlighted as **1** shows the **New Article** button. As if you couldn't guess, this button is what you are going to click on to create a new article.
- The area highlighted as **2** shows the **View & Design Portal** button. Once we have created an article or two, we will be clicking on this button to head to the Designer interface.

- The area highlighted as **3** shows the article summary. It shows the article title, when it was last modified, and the **edit**, **delete**, and **view in portal** links.

- The area highlighted as **4** shows the article editor tools. Here you will find tools to format the content you are creating in the Content Manager. Many will look familiar and give you freedom to create what you need: bulleted lists, numbered lists, text justification, different fonts and colors, and so on. Something else is here in the tools as well, that is, buttons to automatically link different content together. If you click on any of these buttons (**Page Link**, **Article Link**, or **Knowledge Base Link**), a window pops up that shows the specific content you have already created, and automatically creates a link within the current article. Lastly, there is a **Source** button that shows you the HTML source, so if the tools are just not doing it for you, you can go right into the code and make it just the way you want to.

- The area highlighted as **5** shows the **Publish, Cancel, and Delete** buttons. These buttons either publish the page you are creating on the portal, delete the page, or cancel any changes you have made.

The Content Manager is where you can create pages to publish on your User Portal. Honestly, the main strength of the Content Manager is the ability to easily modify existing content in a single interface. You can modify content from one article and move on to the next one with a minimum number of clicks.

So what do we do with this complex content that we create in the Content Manager? Well, we build a fantastic site to publish them on, of course. This is where the Portal Designer comes in. While we create a lot of the content in the Content Manager, the Designer lets you put that content on a site.

If you are still in the Content Manger, let's click on the **View and Design Portal** button; if you are not, just move the cursor over the **Help Desk** link at the top of the page and then **User Portal**, and finally the **Design the User Portal** link.

This is pretty much a WYSIWYG editor for your portal. Let's go over the main sections of this fantastic tool; the numbers mentioned inside the boxes in the preceding screenshot refer to their respective explanation as follows:

- The area highlighted as **1** displays toggles to easily switch from the Designer view to the End User view. This is great because you can immediately see how the users will see the Portal through their web browser without any of the design tools visible.

- In the area highlighted as **2,** you can create a new article or manage content through a pop-up window that allows you to add content on the fly, which you will be using a lot, and you also have the **Preferences** drop-down menu. The **Preferences** dropdown contains both the **Preferences** and **Page Settings** menus. You will be using the **Preferences** menu a lot, unlike the **Page Settings** menu, which just lets you rename your page.

- The area highlighted as **3** displays your tabs or pages that you create to sort different types of information along with the **Jump To** menu that lets you jump on to any other page on your portal. Among some different tabs you might want to put on your portal is the **Home** tab that can be created for users to fill out a Help Desk ticket. The next tab could contain information for new employees (you can name it whatever you heart desires), and the last could be an FAQ that instructs users on how to set up their mobile devices to connect to your e-mail server. The choice is up to you! Don't you just feel that power coursing through your veins? To add a tab, just click on the **New Tab** button and the tab gets added; you just have to name it. Just one thing though, that tab will not be saved until you actually put some content in there. How do you do that? Glad you asked as those buttons are the next things on our list. In the top-left corner is where you can jump to another page you created in the Content Manager.

- The area highlighted as **4** shows your main content section. Articles or knowledge-base pages that either need a lot of information, or are presenting a lot of information should be in this section. For example, this is the spot for pages such as Ticket creation, Company directories, and FAQs.

- The area highlighted as **5** is the sidebar section of your User Portal. Spiceworks is initially laid out with a main section and a secondary one, which is the sidebar on the right-hand side. This is good for shorter snippets of information. You can provide some e-mail links, perhaps a weather forecast, or even a Network Health widget to let your users know that your network is working like it should. What am I saying? Of course, if your network never goes down, you can just disregard that last suggestion.

The Portal Designer is a really powerful design tool that enables you to pretty easily get a site up and running in a minimum amount of time. Before we move on any further, I do have a couple of areas that are deserving of some more in-depth information.

First, let's look at the second highlighted area in the previous image, the **Preferences** button and its drop-down menu.

When we talked about you being able to alter the look and feel of your portal, this is the main area where that happens. You can choose to preset color schemes, add your company logo, name your page, and even do color overrides for different parts of the portal. This is a great and easy tool to make your User Portal look like your own instead of just some cookie cutter. Just make sure to click on the **Save** button before you close it out to make those changes stick.

The second tool that we have to hit before moving on is also in the same highlighted portion of the overview, specifically the **Manage Content** button. I had mentioned earlier that you would be using this a lot, and you will. This is how you add content to pages. Now you might be thinking, "What kind of content can I add?" Well, we are going into that right now. That was kind of spooky how this book just answered the question that you were thinking, right? Just accept it because we are diving into the **Manage Content** button. Go ahead and click away!

Here is just some of the content that you can create on your portal:

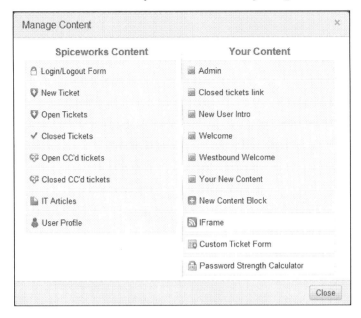

If you notice in the preceding screenshot, the left column is titled as **Spiceworks Content**. This is the content that comes built-in with Spiceworks. The right column is titled as **Your Content**; there are a couple of built-in options such as **iFrame** and **New Content Block** (just adds a new article basically) as well as any pages or articles that you have created.

One of the most important links on this menu is **Custom Ticket Form**. This is a fantastic tool that lets you create forms for creating Help Desk tickets with customized information. You can link Custom Attributes to this form and integrate things such as Department, Priority, or whatever else you wish to add. Just click on it and play around. The interface is very intuitive, and for every feature you add to the form, there is a little gear that shows up which lets you edit the settings for that section.

All in all, a very robust set of tools and options to add different types of content out of the box. Not only that, but as you create more cool articles, they will automatically show up in this menu.

Now, since every organization is different, every User Portal will be different. The information will be set up differently, the FAQ sections will vary, but I can say that one thing all User Portals have in common is a Help Desk ticket creation section. That is one of the reasons we are setting this up, right? So users can log in and open their own tickets along with seeing the status of their open tickets.

Set up the portal the way you think you want it and test it within your team. Get your specific information on pages and experiment with the layout. Log in to the portal and open a ticket or two, and then go in and look through the Spiceworks desktop to see them in the queue. If you do this right now, without finishing this chapter, I can predict with utmost certainty that once you finish this chapter, it will change.

We need to discover a couple of other things that may drastically change the way you look at that ticket-creation section. This portion of the chapter doesn't go into those though. But all is not lost, lucky for you; the next one does highlight one of the main tools we have within Spiceworks to really be able to get some information within Help Desk tickets that means something for us. If you haven't eaten, grab something because the next section shouldn't be read on an empty stomach.

Standard and Custom Attributes

Standard and Custom attributes are fields that you can customize and insert in either a Help Desk ticket or device in your inventory. This is a little more advanced, but we couldn't let it slide because it brings to the table so much functionality. I am not going to dive too deep into this, so here is an overview:

1. First, we need to head to the **Settings** screen. Then move your cursor over the **Help Desk** link at the top of the page, and click on **Settings** on the bottom-left of the menu that opens up.

2. On the **Settings** screen, scroll down to **Advanced and International Options** and click on it. You will find sections for setting up a proxy for your Spiceworks server, Standard Attributes, and Custom Attributes.

Let us first have an overview of the built-in Standard Attributes; we are not going to go through every single one here but just the columns and what they mean. The numbers mentioned inside the boxes in the ensuing screenshot refer to their respective explanation as follows:

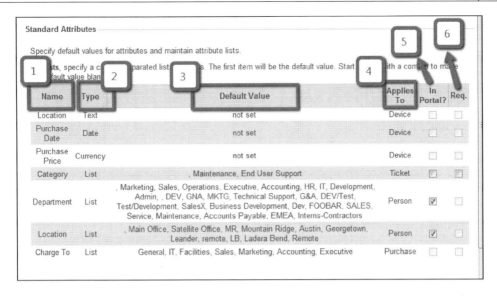

- The area highlighted as **1** displays the **Name** field. It implies the name of the Standard Attribute, and it is not editable.

- The area highlighted as **2** displays the **Type** field. It implies the kind of attribute that this is, and it is also not editable.

- The area highlighted as **3** displays the **Default Value** field. These are the contents of the attribute. If a user needs to modify this value in a ticket or a device, they show up as a drop-down menu. These are editable; just move your cursor over the options, and they will turn yellow. Once they do, just click on them and a text box will appear, where the list was, and you can start editing right away.

- The area highlighted as **4** displays the **Applies To** field. This is a very important attribute. Attributes can apply to devices, people, tickets, vendors, and purchases; it is not editable.

- The area highlighted as **5** displays the **In Portal?** field. This is another very important attribute. Checking this box will allow you to add this attribute to the Custom Ticket form in the User Portal. This attribute is editable.

- The area highlighted as **6** displays the **Req.** field. Checking this box will make this field required when a user is creating a Help Desk ticket through the User Portal. So no more tickets with half filled out forms! A user that tries to submit a Help Desk ticket through the User Portal without this information will receive a message asking them to complete the form before submitting.

Now those are the built-in attributes, which if that were all there were would be cool and help you out. But Spiceworks made it easy for you to create your own custom attributes. These are fully customizable and following is a screenshot of the process of adding one:

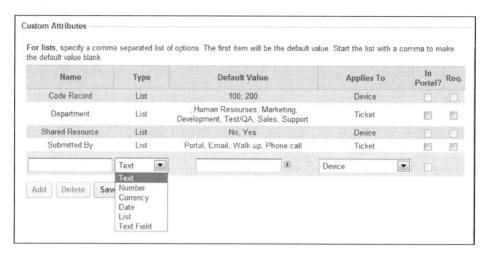

Just scroll down to the Custom Attributes section, click on **Add**, and a new row will open up, which is very similar to how you added Spiceworks users. The columns are the same but I have highlighted the types of attributes you can add. Most are self-explanatory; I just want to highlight something about the **List** option. When adding a list, the values are comma separated with the first value showing up as a default in the dropdown. If you want to create something that is required on the portal, for example, the priority of a ticket, the correct way to do that would be as follows:

```
, low, medium, high
```

This will have a default value of nothing, which means that the user will have to fill that in for them to successfully open a ticket. If you put the values in as low, medium, high, the default value would be low and they could open up a ticket without touching that required attribute. This helps you to get the best results using Custom Attributes.

So you can see how important these attributes can be for you. From filling out the purchase date of a server to what specific area a user is having issues in when they are filling out a ticket through the portal; the possibilities are just about endless. Another great thing about these attributes is that they are all reportable. If you have a list asking a user whether the ticket is in regards to a printing issue (Yes or No), you will be able to pull a report on how may "Yes" tickets there were. So the only limit is how you want to implement these in your Spiceworks installation.

We have been talking a lot about tickets; let's get some created!

Creating a ticket in Spiceworks

There are basically three ways in which tickets get created in Spiceworks:

- **Creating a ticket manually**: A Spiceworks user (not the end user; one of the folks you created earlier in this chapter) creates one manually through the desktop. For end user tickets, this would be for those dreaded **hallway hijacks** where a user stops you in the hallway to tell you about their problem, or a user calls on the phone to tell you there is an issue. Spiceworks admins can also open tickets for tasks, purchases, or change control. The main thing here is that those tickets are directly created within Spiceworks.

- **Creating a ticket through the User Portal**: These tickets will be created through the User Portal when an end user logs into the User Portal and fills out the **Help Desk Ticket** form. Once they click on the **Submit Request** button, a ticket is created and e-mails are furiously sent out to the user (ticket open confirmation) and Spiceworks admins (New Ticket notification).

- **Creating a ticket through the monitored mailbox**: If a user or even a Spiceworks Admin sends an e-mail to the mailbox you configured earlier in this chapter, Spiceworks automatically creates a ticket based on that e-mail. It gleans information from the e-mail itself to create the ticket. As we went over earlier, the sender becomes the creator, the subject becomes the summary, and the body becomes the description. If you already have a mailbox that users send requests to, this will be easy to implement.

You can also configure it to use for a multitude of processes that the IT Dept does on a daily basis. Some examples of this are Change Control, assigning tasks to members of your IT team among a host of others. Now, since most of your user tickets are going to be created through the User Portal by the users themselves or through the monitored mailbox, these tickets have next to no IT Pro interaction. Since there will be times where you need to create a ticket manually, let's go over how to do that now.

1. First click on the **Help Desk** link at the top of the page; this will take you to the Help Desk dashboard.

2. Click on the **New Ticket** button on the top-right part of your screen. A window opens up that looks like the following screenshot:

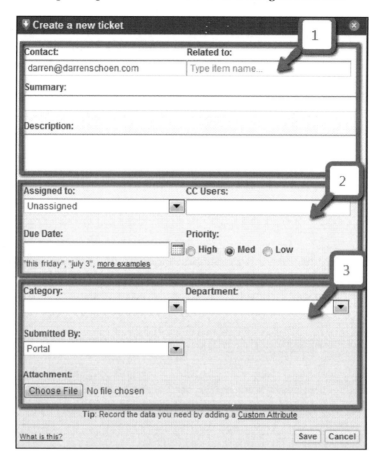

This is the interface where you can manually create a Spiceworks Help Desk ticket. Let's go over some of the important sections; the numbers mentioned inside the boxes in the preceding screenshot refer to their respective explanation as follows:

*   The area highlighted as **1** is the portion of the window that tells you who the ticket creator should be. A great thing about Spiceworks and AD integration (and syncing) is that you can just start typing a name and Spiceworks starts searching for your users giving you a list based on what letters you type. Great for folks like us who spend too much time typing in full names. The **Related to:** field is used if you want to associate this ticket with a specific device. This could be a laptop, desktop, printer, or server. The **Summary:** and **Description:** fields are exactly what they are, that is, a summary of what the ticket is about, and then a longer description of what issue is going on.

- The area highlighted as **2** is where you can immediately assign the ticket to a Help Desk technician, copy someone so they also get updates on the ticket status, put in a due date, and lastly indicate what the priority is. You don't have to assign the ticket to anyone right off the bat, but the option is there for you to do so.

- Now look at the area highlighted as **3** carefully. See anything familiar? No? Are you sure? How about you go back a few pages where we talked about Custom Attributes. Go ahead, skip back, and have a look. Some of those items that we saw in the Custom Attributes section are here in this section. Now, these don't have to show up when you create a ticket yourself; they can also show up this way on the portal so you can have users fill it in before they submit the ticket. They can all be reported on as well. So you want to know how many tickets the Marketing Department created in the past month? You can, and easily too! Now you know why we devoted that precious page space for going through the Custom Attributes section, don't you?

Once you fill everything in, just click on the **Save** button and the ticket is created. Okay, I am going to be a bit candid here. Our goal here is not to have you fill in a lot more fields to open a ticket about a toner being out in the user's printer in the next office. Our goal here is to empower users to fill out their own tickets. Personally, I have not filled out a user issue ticket in quite a while; of course this has come after training my users for many years, but the only tickets I really create are for purchasing and tasks today.

Now opening and working tickets are two different things. Whether you open tickets yourself or the users do it, you are going to need to work through and close them.

Working a Help Desk ticket in Spiceworks

There are two main ways to work a ticket in Spiceworks. If you are wondering what I mean when I say "working" a ticket, this is when you update the status, add information, request more information from a user, add the time worked for, and eventually resolve and close the ticket.

Let's go over the details of what you can do through the Help Desk desktop. Click on the **Help Desk** link at the top of the page to get there. We went over this briefly earlier in this chapter, but now, let me take you deeper into how you can work tickets. Highlight one of the tickets in the queue, and you will see something like the the pane beneath in the following screenshot:

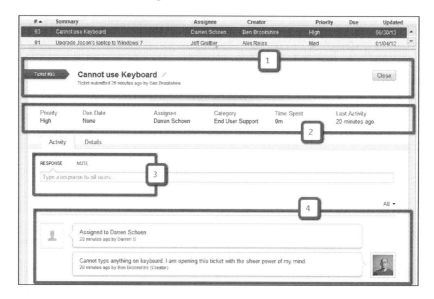

At the top, you see the ticket summary (I didn't highlight it as I know you are smart and could figure out where it was). If there are multiple tickets in the summary portion, the areas below dynamically change to reflect the ticket details when you click on them. There is a lot going on in this small space below the ticket summary list (you might be figuring out that this is a pattern in Spiceworks, that is, lots of information being displayed at one go).

You might also notice the excessive use of the color red in this screenshot. This was not our magic editor marking this one up. If you have a ticket that is a **High** priority, and if you highlight it in the ticket list, it will be red rather than blue to let you know that it needs attention. Let's go through the specifics of what each of these areas in the ticket detail pane do. The numbers mentioned inside the boxes in the preceding screenshot refer to their respective explanation as follows:

- The area highlighted as **1** is where you can edit the ticket summary (just click on the little pencil right next to it). You can also close the ticket by clicking on the **Close** button to the right.

- This portion of the details pane the area highlighted as **2**, is where a lot of the editable information resides: Priority of the ticket, due date, who the ticket is assigned to (**Assignee**), time spent, and when the ticket was worked on last(**Last Activity**). Most of these are editable by clicking on that magic pencil icon next to what you want to modify.

- Right below is another important section the area highlighted as **3**. If you notice, there are two different links in this box, **Response** and **Note**.

  - When you click on **Response** and then type in something directly below, it will be visible to all the users on that ticket. This is great for asking a user for more information as once you type something into that box, Spiceworks will e-mail the update to that user. They then go back to the User Portal and fill in the information you requested, or just reply to the e-mail sent, and Spiceworks updates the ticket.

  - The **Note** functionality is for Spiceworks admins to put a *private* note on the ticket. Only Spiceworks admins will be able to see that information through the Help Desk desktop; it will be invisible to the end users and they will not receive an e-mail saying the ticket was updated.

- The area highlighted as **4** is the activity timeline. Any time a user or Spiceworks Admin touches the ticket, Spiceworks adds what was done to this timeline. This includes closing a ticket so you can exactly see when a ticket was closed.

Spiceworks is constantly working to update their software with the added functionality. Some things on the roadmap are adding purchasing and labour into this pane. There may be enhancements to these views by the time you read this.

But wait a second, isn't there a **Details** tab here that wasn't covered? You are correct! We were just getting to that section of the ticket. Here is a screenshot from the **Details** pane:

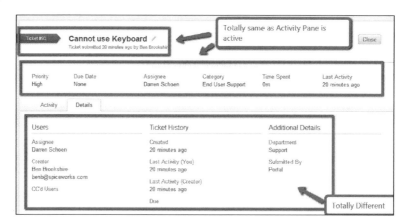

As you switch tabs, the information completely changes. On the **Details** tab, we get some really informational and historical data. At the time of writing this book, you could not edit any of these fields, but it is great that all this information is in one easy place.

We went over how you would lose some functionality of the Help Desk if you didn't have an e-mail connection and a dedicated mailbox earlier. When a ticket is opened, the user gets an e-mail stating that a ticket was opened. When a ticket is assigned, they get an e-mail notifying them as well. Whenever something is typed in the **Response** box, the user gets it in their inbox. If you have set up a dedicated mailbox, they can then just reply to the e-mail with their response and Spiceworks updates the timeline automatically. This is great for IT Professionals who are not present at their computer desk a lot and are running around their facility taking care of users, or on the road and don't have access to a machine with Spiceworks. So without a dedicated mailbox that Spiceworks can use, all of that goes away. So you see, having one is very important.

Tickets can be opened, updated, information requested, information given, and closed through e-mail. Yes, you can even close tickets via this method. In fact, you can add time, assign tickets, create tickets, and do almost everything you can do through the desktop with the Spiceworks Help Desk software called, Tickets Anywhere.

When you e-mail the monitored mailbox with specific commands in the body of the e-mail, Spiceworks reads those and does tasks based on those commands. They are preceded by a hashtag and following are a few examples:

Action	Commands
Close a ticket	• `#close`
Set the priority of a ticket	• `#priority high`
	• `#priority low`
Accept a ticket	• `#accept`
	• `#assign to me`

These are just a few examples; the complete list can be found at : `http://community.spiceworks.com/help/Tickets_Anywhere`.

As you can see, this is a really powerful tool you can use to keep your users happy. No more coming back to your desk and finding e-mails and voicemails sent earlier by the users that day; you can immediately respond to their requests. In my environment, this has increased the satisfaction of our end users as they get immediate notifications during the different phases of resolving an issue.

Mobile clients

Spiceworks also has mobile clients for iOS and Android that give quite a lot of functionality. One thing about them though, you have to be on the network that you have installed Spiceworks on. If you are on the road and connected through your cellular network, without a VPN connection to your internal network, you are out of luck with the mobile clients. If you do have an internal Wi-Fi throughout your facility, the Spiceworks application would be a good fit.

That's it for working tickets! You have learned that you can work them from just about anywhere if you have some kind of data connection and e-mail connectivity, or a Wi-Fi connection with the mobile client.

There is one last thing we need to go over before we move to the next chapter.

Extending the User Portal and Help Desk using plugins

One of the greatest things about Spiceworks is how users have extended the functionality of the main application using plugins. There are literally hundreds of them in the Spiceworks community that you can download and install right from the application itself. We are going to go over this in more detail in *Chapter 5, Taking Spiceworks to the Next Level*, but I wanted to touch on the plugins that come out of the box with the help desk.

Open up the Help Desk desktop (if you are not sure how to do it, just click on the **Help Desk** link at the top of the page), and then click on the **Settings** button on the right-hand side above the ticket summary pane.

We have been here before configuring who receives an e-mail when an event occurs within a ticket. I want you to focus on the **Help Desk Extensions** section for this final portion of the chapter. The two plugins that are included during install are My Ticket Rules and My Ticket Views. We talked about the My Ticket Views plugin briefly, but I want to get into the My Ticket Rules plugin right now.

Once you move your cursor over the My Ticket Rules plugin, an **Edit** button comes up; let's click on it. A window will open up with the existing rules, or you can choose to create a new one by clicking on the button at the bottom that is surprisingly called **Add Rule**. This screen will slide into the window as follows:

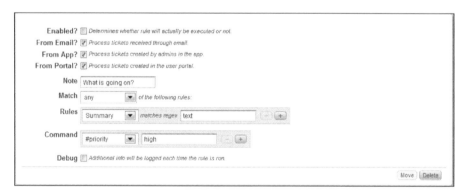

This is a really powerful toolset by which you can configure Spiceworks to automatically perform a set of tasks based on a set of criteria:

- The top portion defines whether the rule is enabled and also whether to process based on where the ticket was generated from (application, e-mail, or portal). This is great as you can filter out any tickets that are created through the application itself if you choose.

- Next, the **Note** portion is to describe what the rule is for.
- The **Match** section just defines whether Spiceworks matches any or all of the rules that are defined in the next section.
- For the **Rules** section, you can choose many options, e-mail address, summary, description, created by, and so on from the drop-down menu.

Many of the fields within the ticket itself are present here. Within my environment, we have a rule that if our CEO or CFO opens a ticket, it is automatically set to a high priority. You can really do a lot here, and like a lot of the plugins, this really extends the functionality of Spiceworks. We will be doing more of a deep dive into plugins in *Chapter 5, Taking Spiceworks to the Next Level*; so if you liked what you saw here, there is definitely more to come.

Summary

Wow! You made it through—configuring the Help Desk and User Portal. There was a lot of information in this chapter, and since you are reading this, you got through and learned a few things in the process. You should be at least familiar with creating content and designing the User Portal, setting up your help desk for e-mail, creating and working tickets, and setting those Custom Attributes. There could be many books written on just what we covered here, so if you want to dive a little deeper or have additional questions on what we went through, here is a helpful link:

`http://community.spiceworks.com/help/#Helpdesk`

So if you have any tweaks you want to do on your portal, configure Custom Attributes or tickets you want to create; do it now (getting a refreshing beverage and snack is also allowed). The next chapter is dedicated to a lot of the other features within Spiceworks: reporting, purchasing, and alerts are all covered along with many more. That's right, we've barely scratched the surface on all the things Spiceworks can do. So get ready, because here we go!

4
Configuring Other Spiceworks Features

In Spiceworks, the Help Desk and network inventory get all the attention but there are many other features within the app that can make your IT days easier. Each of them is tightly integrated with the other parts of the app. Some of the features we are going to cover in this chapter allow you to slice and dice the data within Spiceworks to provide easy-to-digest information, some compliment other parts of the app, and some can even help make considerable savings in your IT budget.

Without further ado, the following are the topics we will cover in this chapter:

- Reporting in Spiceworks
- Network Monitoring and Alerts in Spiceworks
- Purchasing through Spiceworks
- Mobile device management in Spiceworks
- Other Spiceworks features

We have a lot to cover, all of it awesome, so let's jump right in!

Reporting in Spiceworks

There really isn't anything more annoying than non-tech folks asking us for data that they could easily get themselves again and again. We are expected to be some kind of wizard supporting our users, keeping our infrastructure up, and providing them with colourful graphs and charts. Crazy, right? What if there was a way to automate some of this reporting? Well, there is a way through Spiceworks.

Spiceworks has a robust reporting engine out of the box. It contains loads of built-in templates, and you can create your own right through the Spiceworks interface. You can even import reports directly from the always active Spiceworks Community. If you have a proprietary system that no other report covers, use Spiceworks to support native SQL reporting. So, if you are an SQL guru, you can work your magic here.

You can also give non-IT staff access to Spiceworks as a reporting user so they cannot see Inventory, Help Desk, or anything else except the reports you assign. Doesn't it sound too good to be true? It isn't. Let's go through how to set it up.

To get to the reporting interface, just mouse over either **Inventory** or **Help Desk** links at the top of any page in the app. There is a **Reporting** link right above the **Settings** link on the right side. This will take you to the reporting interface, as shown in the next screenshot:

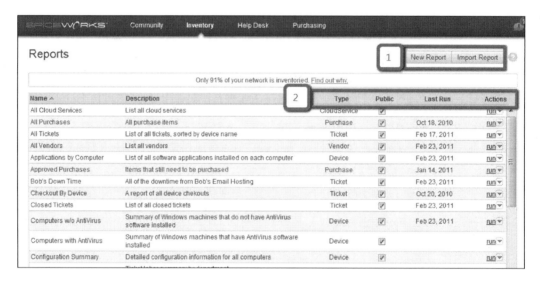

Spiceworks comes with quite a few very useful reports. The interface is pretty straightforward, but for now let's go through a couple of areas that are of interest.

1. The area highlighted as **1** displays buttons that allow you to either open the **New Report** screen or import a report file from your local machine. You will be using the **New Report** a lot; we will be getting into building reports very soon in this chapter.

2. The top bar along your **Reports** interface has great information. We didn't highlight the **Name** or **Description** columns as you probably know what those are. Let's briefly go over the area highlighted as **2**:

   ° **Report Type**: This tells you what dataset this report corresponds to. **Tickets**, **Purchases**, and **Devices** are all options. If you build your report in SQL, the SQL is displayed up here.

   ° **Public**: This tells you if a reporting user can see it or only Spiceworks admins can.

   ° **Last Run**: The last time this report was run.

   ° **Actions**: In this drop-down menu you will find the various things that you can do with a report. Some of these include **Edit**, **Run**, **Share**, and so on.

Let's talk about the **Action** menu. You will be utilizing this a lot as you use Spiceworks Reporting. If you mouse over the **run** link, a new menu materializes:

- **Run**: This option is used to run the report
- **Edit**: This option is used to modify the report
- **Share**: This option is used for sharing the report on Spiceworks Community
- **Export**: This option is used for exporting the report to your local machine
- **Delete**: This option is used to delete the report

Let's run a built-in report and look at the results. Pick any report you want, and then just click on the **run** link in the far right column. The following screenshot will appear as the result screen:

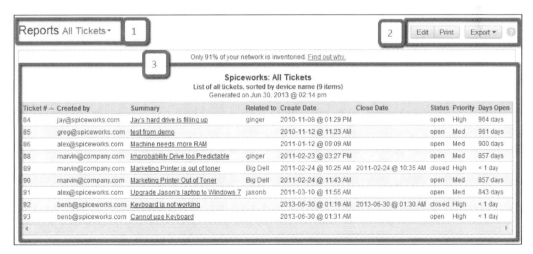

This is a pretty straightforward interface, but there are some hidden gems, let's go over them. as shown in the following steps:

1. The area highlighted as **1** are links to not only the **Reports** main screen but also to every report you have currently installed in your Spiceworks installation. If you click on the **Report name** right next to the bold typeface **Reports** link, a drop-down list will appear with all reports you have, and you can easily jump from one report to another.

2. The area highlighted as **2** you can **Edit**, **Print**, or **Export** the current report. The **Edit** button will take you back to the **Report Creator** screen with all respective fields filled in for this output. The **Print** button allows you to print your reports. Finally you have the **Export** button. This allows you to export your report into three formats: PDF, CSV, and EXCEL. Very handy indeed!

3. The area highlighted as **3** you will find the result of the report. In the preceding example, we run a report that queried Help Desk Tickets. Notice that for each row, those results are clickable, taking you directly to the Help Desk item that it referenced. Most reports are like this in Spiceworks. They are interactive where you can directly go to the resources by just clicking on the row in the report.

Ok, we have gone over the Reporting interface, run a built-in report, and seen what it looks like. Let's now create a brand new report. If you are still on an individual report screen, just click on the **Reports** button shown in the preceding screenshot. Once you are there, click on the **New Report** button, and Spiceworks presents you with their **Report Builder** interface:

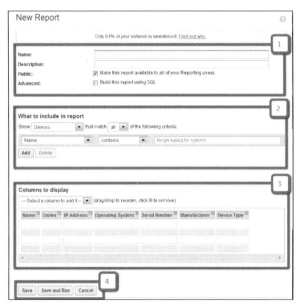

As you must have figured out by now, many creation tools in Spiceworks look very simple but have the ability to create some complex information. This interface is no different. Let's go through the main portions. as shown in the following steps:

1. In the area highlighted as **1** you enter the name of your report and a good description. You can also decide if you want the report to be **Public**, meaning all Spiceworks admins and reporting users will see it, or if you decide not to check that box, only Spiceworks admins will have access to it. Here you can choose to write the report in SQL as well. If you do decide this is the way to go, the fields following this will change into a SQL console.

2. **What to Include in report**: In the area highlighted as **2** looks so simple, yet you can really extract complex data sets from it. Here you define what you want in the report. If you need workstations with 2 GB RAM and no antivirus, or if you want a list of all workstations with a certain piece of software where the report tells you location, IP Address, and what user logged in last, it can be done here. The possibilities are only limited by your imagination and if you don't have the data in your Spiceworks DB.

3. **Columns to display**: So you have your dataset all done. You have narrowed down a tangled mess into a clean subset. Unless you can design how it looks and how the data is presented, it does you no good. The area highlighted as 3 is where you can do that. Add, remove, and modify columns at your whim.

4. **Save** options: The area highlighted as **4** you can either choose **Save** to save the report without running it, **Save and Run** to save and run the report, or if you have made a mistake, you can just click on **Cancel** to cancel out of the **Report Creator**.

This is a pretty robust report creation tool. As told earlier, if you are an SQL guru, you can write reports in SQL as well. With some tinkering, you can even get products such as Crystal Reports to work with Spiceworks. The last option of using a third-party reporting tool requires some serious Spiceworks expertise, so we won't be covering it in this book. A quick search on the Spiceworks Community will reveal this process.

Did someone say Spiceworks Community? Now, we are all really busy people. You don't have hours of your day to come up with reports for every single thing on your network. Odds are someone else has already written a report that if not fully suits your needs, fulfills 90 percent of them. These are all in the Spiceworks Community, and free for you to install. Let's go back to the main **Reports** screen. Under the installed reports pane is a **Featured Community Reports** pane. There are several reports here that you can install, and some might be useful to you. These are only a small fraction of what is out in the Spiceworks Community though.

For more information on the *Shared Reports* article of the Spiceworks Community, refer to `http://community.spiceworks.com/reports`. When you visit this URL, a screen as shown in the following screenshot will appear:

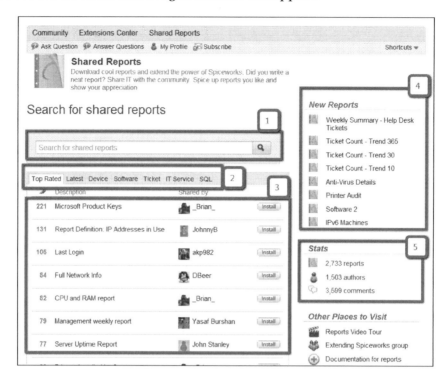

This is such a great resource for you to get the reports you need:

- The area highlighted as **1** a **Search** bar so you can easily search for a report on a certain thing.

- The tabs in the area highlighted as **2** sort the shared reports in different ways. Some are by category (for example, **IT Service**, **Software**, or **SQL**), some are by date uploaded to the Community (for example, **Latest**), and the default when you arrive is the **Top Rated**. Users on the community (and you are one now!) can Spice up a report if they like it, so these are the highest rated for all uploaded reports.

- When you click on a tab in the area highlighted as **2**, the reports that correspond to that tab show up the area highlighted as **3**. By default, they will be sorted based on their spice rating that is in the far left column. Next is the **Description** of the report, the author, and the **Install** button. We will be going over how to install right after this list, so hang on.

- The area highlighted as **4 New Reports** pane, where you can see the newest reports uploaded to the community by users like yourself.

- At the time of this writing, there were over 2700 shared reports in the **Shared Reports Stats**. You should be able to find something you can use in all those the area highlighted as **5**!

So, whether you search for a report you want, or just pick one out of the **Top Rated** list, now the question is how to get that report into your Spiceworks Install. The following steps show how you complete this complex process:

1. For whatever report you want to install, click on the **Install** button, as shown in the previous screenshot.

2. Your screen will blink for a moment, and then you should be taken to your local Spiceworks **Report** screen.

3. Run the report.

That was tough right? Seriously though, Spiceworks couldn't make it much simpler to install shared reports into your local installation.

Well, we have seen how to run, create, and even install reports. *Chapter 5*, *Taking Spiceworks to the Next Level*, goes into a little more depth on sharing reports you create, but for now we need to move to the next section *Network Monitoring and Alerts in Spiceworks*!

Network monitoring and alerts in Spiceworks

So you have learned that Spiceworks has some effective Inventory capabilities, a robust Help Desk, and even does reporting on all their data. Also, Spiceworks has some built-in monitoring and alerting capabilities. Disk space, printer toner, connectivity, hardware changes, or even when a specific piece of software is installed, they can all be monitored and an alert sent out when a condition is met.

There are a ton of these alerts built-in, let's have a look at what Spiceworks comes with and how to set up your own.

Go to the **Settings** page and then click on the **Monitors and Alerts** link.

You will be taken to the main **Monitors and Alerts** page. Here you can take a look at all the monitors and alerts that are installed with Spiceworks. The interface should look pretty familiar to you from the different areas of Spiceworks we have gone through already. In the first section, the columns are as follows:

- **Name**: In this column, enter the name of Monitor/Alert.
- **Description**: In this column, enter the description of Monitor/Alert.
- **Applies To**: This column describes what the Monitor/Alert applies to
- **Email**: This box refers to Spiceworks Admin users and e-mail alerts. Checking this box will instruct Spiceworks to automatically e-mail any Spiceworks Admin user that has the **Alerts** box checked under their e-mail settings. Uncheck this box to disable e-mail for this Monitor/Alert.
- **On**: Checking this box means this Monitor/Alert will be active.
- **Edit**: Just as the **Reports** screen, this is a drop-down to either edit or delete Monitor/Alert.

You can click on the **Edit** link for any of these Monitor/Alert, and the settings will appear within the pane itself. At the bottom of the list of alerts, there is a link that lets you build your own Alert. Let's click on that link and start creating an Alert/Monitor:

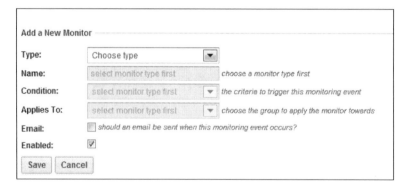

If you notice, only the **Type** field can be chosen when you open this menu. Go ahead and click on the drop-down and see all the options you have here. Once you click on one of these, the rest of the fields will open up with prefilled suggestions. For example, if you choose **Disk** in the first field, you will get the following configuration:

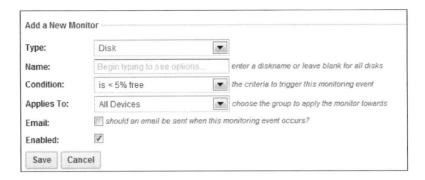

Go ahead and play around with these alerts and see what will work for you. Remember when we set up specific groups within our network inventory? Well, you can set these alerts to specifically monitor those groups. If you have set up any, look in the **Applies To:** drop-down and they will be there. This is great for specific machines you need to monitor more frequently than the daily full scan. You can really get specific with the use of custom groups, custom attributes, and alerts. It helps you to be much more proactive rather than reactive. You can monitor the following with this tool, and remember this is just a small sample of what you can do:

- Tracking changes in desktop hardware
- Tracking software licenses and updates
- Web traffic monitoring
- Network load monitoring
- Up/down monitoring for websites and servers

A full list of what can be monitored can be found at the following link:

```
http://community.spiceworks.com/help/Setting_Up_Monitors_And_Email_
Alerts
```

Once you have the alert you want, just click on **Save**, and it will show up in the preceding list.

Finally, you need to choose what e-mail server you want these alerts to go out on. These options are placed after the list of alerts that are already configured, as shown in the following screenshot:

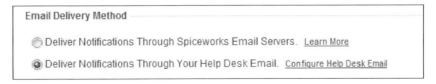

There are two options in the preceding screenshot:

- **Deliver Notifications Through Spiceworks Email Servers**: This option will route all notifications from the alerts and monitors through Spiceworks e-mail servers. This can be as handy because if you are monitoring your internal e-mail server, and it goes down, you would never get an alert because Spiceworks uses it to send out alerts. If this option is checked, your local Spiceworks install will use the Spiceworks company e-mail servers basically as SMTP servers when it sends alert e-mails out.

- **Deliver Notifications Through your Help Desk Email** Selecting this option, you will be able to use your own internal e-mail servers to send out alerts.

 In the preceding screenshot, all your Help Desk notification e-mails will still go out on whatever e-mail server you configured within your Spiceworks install. This only applies to alerts.

So that's our overview of Monitoring and Alerts in Spiceworks. Since this is more of a rapid-fire chapter, we are going to get right on to purchasing in Spiceworks so we can show you how to save some money!

Purchasing features in Spiceworks

Spiceworks provides a whole purchasing ecosystem between the application and the Community. It lets you set up a purchasing process and even helps you get multiple quotes for what you need. In addition, Spiceworks keeps a record of what you purchase and you can report on it. If you want to know how much you spent on a toner in the last year, Spiceworks can do it!

Now let's move on to the purchasing feature in the Spiceworks app. Hover your mouse over the **Purchasing** link at the top of any page within the app, and then click on **Purchase List**.

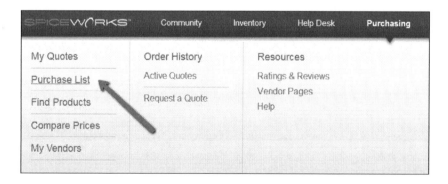

This is going to bring us to our **Purchase List**. You can see in the following screenshot that there are many items. On your install, the list will be empty because you haven't added any purchases to your Spiceworks install yet.

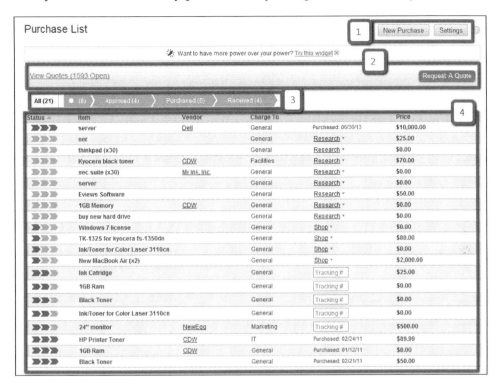

This is the screen where some of the Spiceworks Purchasing magic happens. Let's take a look at some of the important areas as mentioned in the following steps:

1. The area highlighted as **1** displays the **New Purchase** and **Settings** buttons. If you click on the **Settings** button, it will take you to the **Purchasing Settings** page where you can set a monthly budget along with a few other options. We will be going over this in more detail later in the chapter.

2. The area highlighted as **2** deals with your quotes that you get from Spiceworks. Spiceworks has an automatic **Request A Quote** system where you can get quotes from different vendors.

3. The area highlighted as **3** describes the purchasing process within Spiceworks and how to move purchases that you create along. There are four stages of a purchase in this process:

   ○ **Pending**: Once you create a purchase, the far left part of these icons will turn green. When you see this in the purchase list, it will show up as **Research**, which is a link that you can click on to open up the Spiceworks Community to research your purchase. A purchase needs to be approved to move to the next step.

   ○ **Approved**: Spiceworks assumes you have found the item you want and the purchase has been approved. When you see this in the purchase list, it will show up a **Shop** link where you can compare prices or even shop right from the Spiceworks app. A purchase needs to be purchased to move to the next step.

   ○ **Purchased**: So now Spiceworks assumes you have bought this item. When you see this in the purchase list, there will be a box where you can input a tracking number. A purchase needs to be received to move to the next step.

   ○ **Received**: Once this has been activated, Spiceworks closes this purchase. When you see these in the **Purchase List**, the date it was purchased is displayed.

4. The area highlighted as **4** displays a list of all purchases you entered into Spiceworks. As you can see, they are all in different stages of the purchase process. Vendor information, product information, and even what department you want to charge it to can be in different columns along with the amount of purchase.

Let's quickly go through how to start a purchase as well as how to do a Request For Quote.

Just click on the **New Purchase** button, as highlighted in the previous screenshot in step 1. This will open up the **Create a new purchase** window, as shown in the following screenshot:

This is pretty standard information for whatever you purchase. Things such as for whom it was purchased, quantity, and possible vendor are all included. Note that you can associate a purchase with a user within Spiceworks as well.

Once you have entered all your data, just click on **Save**, and it will show up in your purchase list; you can move it along the Spiceworks Purchase process.

One last thing about purchasing in Spiceworks. Have you ever needed multiple quotes for an item that you are buying? Depending on the industry you are in, you may need three quotes for most items you need to buy! Spiceworks has a great system called **Request For Quote** (**RFQ**) where you can get quotes from several different vendors without spending a lot of time.

In the screenshot describing the **Purchase List**, you can see an orange button labeled **Request A Quote** at the top right of the **Purchase List** window. Clicking on that will take you to the Spiceworks Community where you can request quotes from different vendors. It can save you a lot of time and get a great price as well!

That's all we can fit in about Spiceworks purchasing. We will be looking at other Spiceworks features in a very short span of time, so you might want to grab a stimulating beverage as this is going to go quick!

Mobile Device Management in Spiceworks

So, how are you managing your mobile devices on your network? **Bring Your Own Device (BYOD)** is the rage at the moment, causing headaches for IT staff everywhere. Tablets, phones and user laptops are being brought on to your network, the challenge you have is how do you manage your company's data on these devices?

Spiceworks recently added **Mobile Device Management (MDM)** into the app. Such apps have limited control over mobile clients (phones, tablets) right from an administrative console. Some controls that are being implemented are as follows:

- The ability to remotely wipe the device of all data
- The ability to change the passcode to get into the device
- The ability to distribute apps right to the device
- The ability to locate the device

To get started with this, just mouse over the **Inventory** link at the top of any page in the app, and click on **Mobile Devices**. You will now see the following screenshot:

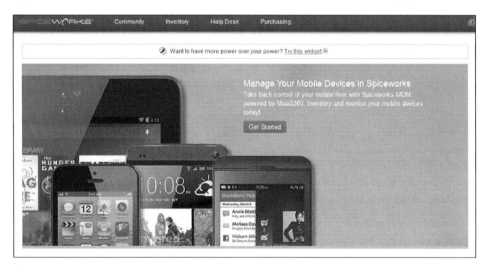

There are a plethora of clients out there that offer varying levels of control for mobile devices, and Spiceworks does it in partnership with MaaS360. Does that sound good to you? Then you are in the right place. Just click on the blue **Get Started** button seen in the preceding screenshot, and you will be off on your Spiceworks MDM journey.

 If you are currently using MaaS360, Spiceworks will integrate right into your current administrative console.

The Mobile Device Management within Spiceworks is brand new. As with all the other features within the app, they will continue to improve on this service and add features. That's all we have for MDM, let's continue our lightning round with some other Spiceworks features.

Other Spiceworks features

In this section, we are going to give you a high-level overview of several other Spiceworks features. We are going to learn a lot about them in the next few sections to whet your appetite.

Spiceworks Knowledge Base

Most IT pros know that one of the keys to quickly resolving issues that arise is having a good Knowledge Base handy. In case you don't know, a Knowledge Base is a repository of solutions to complex issues, tricks about resolving common issues, and useful How-To's. Spiceworks provides one when you install the app and gives you access to thousands of existing articles shared by the Spiceworks Community members. You can edit these articles to suit your unique environment, and then save them. To get there, just mouse over the **Inventory** link on top of any page in the app and click on the **Knowledge Base** link from the **Navigation** menu.

You will be presented with your very own Knowledge Base, as shown in the following screenshot:

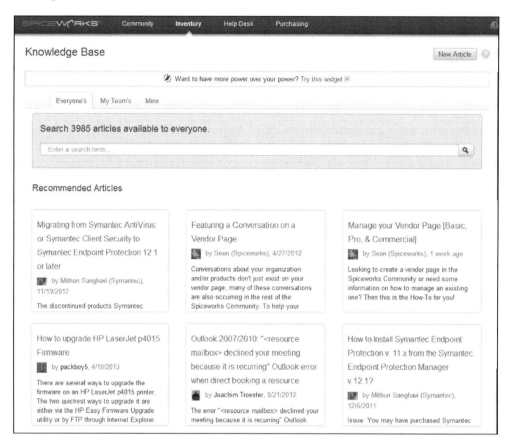

When you first open the **Knowledge Base**, there will be several recommended articles which will be selected based on what kind of devices you have in your network inventory. These recommended articles change as your network changes, so keep checking back for new suggestions.

There are several ways to share these articles and they can be seen in the following screenshot:

If you notice the highlighted portion in the preceding screenshot, there are three buttons:

- **Share**: When you hover your mouse over this button, it tells you who that article is currently shared with. Clicking on this button will allow you to share with your team of Spiceworks admins, publish directly to your user portal, and share with the community (although any article that you get from the Spiceworks Community will already be shared there). You can also add the e-mail addresses in a field and invite people to collaborate on rewriting it for your own use.

- **Copy and Edit**: Clicking on this button opens a page where you can edit the entire article to suit your own needs, and then save it.

- **Bookmark**: Clicking this will bookmark this article in the **Mine** tab on your Knowledge Base so you can come back to it later.

There are numerous articles out there on every conceivable topic. Do a quick search and you will be impressed.

Spiceworks cloud services dashboard

We have talked a lot and focused mostly on traditional devices that reside on your physical network. Spiceworks scans and monitors them very well. But the IT infrastructure of today also resides in the cloud. Many organizations have chosen to host e-mail, file services, and even virtual machines not on premises, but out in the cloud.

Spiceworks knows this and has set up a cloud services dashboard where you can monitor usage and stats from many cloud providers that you may currently have.

As an IT pro, you need to stay proactive in addressing any possible issues, especially if you cannot physically resolve them yourself. That is where Spiceworks and its cloud services dashboard come in.

After a successful scan, Spiceworks will most likely detect some of these if any of them are connected to your current infrastructure that it is scanning. All you need to do is provide credentials for Spiceworks to log into your cloud provider, and it will grab stats and other information.

To get to this dashboard, just open the **Inventory** navigation menu and click on the **Cloud Services** link. If Spiceworks has detected anything on your network, it will show up here. To add one, just click on the **Add** button and a window will pop up where you can choose one of the supported providers, and then enter your login credentials. The current list for supported providers is as follows:

- Rackspace Cloud and Email: This is a popular cloud services provider
- Office 365: This is Microsoft's solution for cloud services
- Google Apps: This is Google's suite for various online cloud services
- Mozy: This is a cloud backup solution
- Dropbox: This is cloud backup, file transfer service
- My ISP: This will monitor your bandwidth from your ISP

This page provides you with a simple and easy interface to see any of the cloud service providers you have in your environment. Spiceworks monitors these services and even provides stats such as uptime and mailbox space used for many of them. Spiceworks is adding new providers all the time; if the one you use is not on there, it may be soon. Speaking of the cloud, let's talk about the network map in the next section.

Using the network map in Spiceworks

There is a saying that a picture is worth a thousand words. This is also true for a visually rendered version of your network. The network map takes the information it collects and graphically represents it in an interactive format. With this cool tool, you can see your network infrastructure in all its glory (or dismay, depending on your network). There are a couple of views that you can render:

- **Backbone**: This view shows you the backbone of your network. It also highlights hotspots and presents groups of devices as a cloud. This is a great way of tracking what groups of devices are taking up a ton of bandwidth and even narrowing it down to specific machines.
- **All Devices**: This view shows everything on your network. Depending on how large your network is, this can be a bit overwhelming.

To get to your Network Map, just open the **Inventory** navigation menu and click on **Network Map**. This will open up the **Network Map** interface and ask you if you want to view either the **Backbone** or **All Devices** view.

Spiceworks also graphically represents devices and network pipes in a few different ways as follows:

- **Cloud**: This represents a network of similar devices and helps in making the network map less cluttered. To drill down into the devices of a particular cloud on your network map, just click on it and they will expand.

- **Thick and thin lines**: These lines represent higher and lower bandwidth connections.

- **Red line**: This line represents a network connection that is at least 75 percent utilized.

- **Yellow line**: This line represents a network connection that is at least 50 percent utilized.

Once in network map, you can move it around and even edit information on certain devices. Not all network switches are currently supported, but more are being added with every release.

Summary

We have covered a boatload of information in this chapter. If you are a little overwhelmed, don't worry, most IT pros feel that way the first time they see what Spiceworks can do. It is suggested that you explore around Spiceworks. There is a lot more that we couldn't get to in this book that is in the app. You have kept up with us on this journey and we are almost complete.

The next chapter talks about how to really go to the next level in Spiceworks by leveraging the Spiceworks Community. We have talked about it a lot, but we really dig in and show you some of the power that is there and how you can use it to make your day easier! Ready or not, we are going there anyway!

5
Taking Spiceworks to the Next Level

Welcome to the final chapter of this book. Our goal when we started was to get you a working install and to highlight some features within the Spiceworks app. If we did our job right, right now you should have a very functional Spiceworks install and also have learned a ton.

Network inventory, help desk, purchasing, basic reporting, asset management, and much more has been covered up to this point; but the crazy thing is we haven't even gone over all of the Spiceworks functionalities, or how you can use it in your environment. In this chapter, we will give you some tools to take your knowledge of Spiceworks to the next level. You may ask, "What is the next level?" Well, that is up to you! First, Spiceworks is such a rich application and in its short existence has evolved very rapidly. From a very early iteration, although it has not been open source, the company has welcomed plugins and hosted the most vibrant SMB IT community on the Web. There is a wealth of knowledge on that community that can, not only instruct you on how to configure Spiceworks exactly to your needs, but also how to create some of these tools. As you get more fluent with how Spiceworks functions, you can contribute to help someone else too!

We will also be going over how you can meet other Spiceworks users in the real world. Whether it be a local user group, in-person training or SpiceWorld (user conference), users of Spiceworks don't just connect from their desks, they do it in the real world as well.

Let's get right into it by starting with the Spiceworks community.

A little bit about the community itself. From the very beginning, the Spiceworks community has been part of the app. Initially, it was a place for feature requests by users, but as the app grew, the community grew along with it. At the time of this writing, there are 567 forums on just about every IT topic. There are also 116 user groups, what Spiceworks calls **SpiceCorps**, where IT pros like you get together and not just talk about Spiceworks, but have presentations by vendors and get feedback from others on the challenges they have. Lastly, there are more than 1,600 of what are called **vendor pages**. These are pages that vendors and companies set up to get directly involved with the Spiceworks community and users themselves.

You may be familiar with connecting into the community; if you're not, just click on the **Community** link at the top-right portion of your screen. You will find yourself at the front page of the community. Any time you log into your Spiceworks install, you will also be logging yourself into the community; all you have to do is click on the link at the top of the page. You will see your username in the upper right-hand corner of the window. Now mouse over it and click on the **My Profile** link to open your profile page. If you belong to one of the myriad of social networks out there, some of this may look familiar to you. Let's go over the different areas:

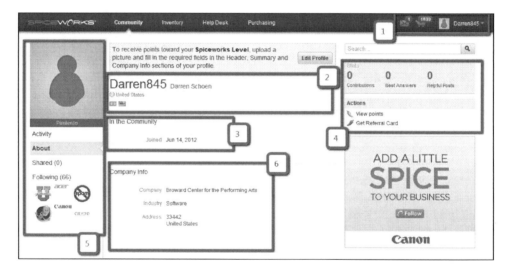

- The area highlighted as **1** is where you will find your community username, your outstanding quotes, and your private message inbox link. If you mouse over your username, a menu opens (how you got here in the first place) from where you can also log out, see your account settings, and get help.

- The area highlighted as **2** shows your community username as the rest of the community will see it, your real name, location, and a section where the Spiceworks community awards badges. In this example, we have the version of Spiceworks you first installed and a country flag.

- The area highlighted as **3** is where your group affiliations show up along with the date you first joined the Spiceworks community.

- The area highlighted as **4** tallies how many contributions you have in the community, how many best answers, and how many helpful posts. There are two links under those and they are as follows:

    ○ **View Points**: This takes you to your **Community Points** profile page. Everything you do in the community earns you points. They are not good for much of anything except differentiating those new to the community and those that have been active for quite a while. The more points you get, the spicier the pepper that shows up under your profile pic. We will be getting into the points in the next section of this chapter.

    ○ **Get Referral Card**: This takes you to a page where you can print out cards to give out to folks to tell them about Spiceworks. Each user can refer people and if they download and install Spiceworks, the referring user gets some community points.

- The area highlighted as **5** is where your profile pic shows up, directly under your pepper level, and beneath that is your navigation pane for your profile on the community. The labels are pretty self-explanatory. **Activity** means your recent activity: posts, comments, and what topics you have voted Spicy. **About** is the page you are on, it is all about you. **Shared** shows the content you have created and uploaded to the community: plugins, reviews, reports, scripts, and the like. Directly below **Shared** are the IT pros and companies names that you are currently following and that are following you.

- The area highlighted as **6** is your company info. If you have filled any of it in, it will show up here.

Now this page is pretty sparse since you are new to the community. Let's look at one that is a bit more filled in!

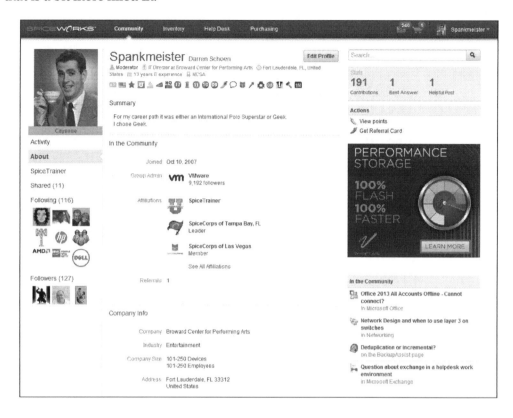

Look at that dashing fellow in the preceding screenshot. He must be an IT rockstar! OK, a little bit of humor there, this is my community page. Feel free to look me up when you get on the community!

A hot topic on any social network is privacy. How much of your information can others see on your page and how do you keep anything sensitive under lock and key? Spiceworks is great about this, let's go through how you can either lock your community profile down, or leave it wide open; the choice is yours!

Let's get to your **Settings** page so we can take care of your privacy on social networking sites. As you are now on your profile page, move your mouse over your username in the upper-right corner and click on **Account Settings**. You will see something very similar to the following screenshot:

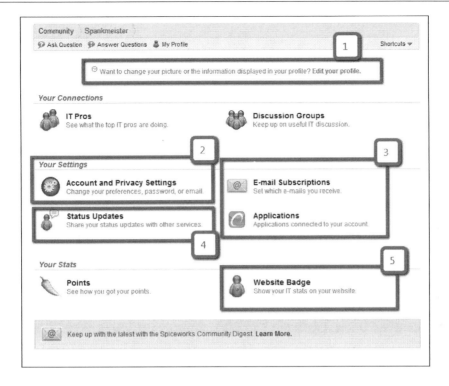

Let's discuss the various sections of this screenshot in brief:

- The area highlighted as **1** is where you can easily edit your profile. Just click on the link to modify your community username, real name, company information, your certifications, skills, and interests. We won't get into it deeper as I know you are a very smart IT pro and can figure it out on your own.

- The area highlighted as **2** is the **Account and Privacy Settings** page. We are going into this a little deeper, but here is where the catch is.

- The area highlighted as **3** is where you can see if any applications are connected to your account through your Spiceworks install and also see your e-mail subscriptions. E-mail subscriptions are easily unsubscribed to. Yes, it is true.

- The area highlighted as **4** is where you can connect your Spiceworks status updates to your Twitter feed.

- Lastly, the area highlighted as **5** is where you can get some custom website badges to put up on your site. There are some nifty ones here that even have your Spiceworks username and profile pics embedded within them!

Since we are here to talk about privacy, let's click on that link now. This opens a page that allows you to change your community password, lets you specify your time zone, whether you want to automatically subscribe to any topic you reply to and an option to either let your quotes be shared or not. Next, we will discuss privacy in detail.

> *Privacy*
>
> Specify who can see your personal info (full name, company information, etc). **Preview your profile** with this info hidden.
>
> ○ Only me and Spiceworks employees.
>
> ○ Only people I follow.
>
> ● Only SpiceHeads that are **Poblano** or higher. (Default)
>
> ○ Everyone else (including logged out guests).
>
> Save

There are several options here, the top being the most restrictive and the bottom having no restrictions. You can also preview each setting. The option I have checked in the preceding screenshot is a smart choice. With this restriction of a user needing to be at a certain level within the community before any of his/her information is shared, only IT pros who are active in the community can see it.

You may wonder about Spiceworks' privacy policy regarding spam and e-mail addresses. I know I did when I first installed Spiceworks. From my experience of over six years of them having my e-mail and personal information, they do not spam you with things that you do not sign up for. As an IT pro, I have signed up on many sites only to get 7,036,720,847 e-mails from the site on a daily basis. Now, if you sign up for every category there is, you will get quite a few e-mails a month. But if you sign up for only one category, they will not add you to others without your consent.

Connecting with other IT pros and vendors

One of the great things about the community is that you can easily connect with both other IT pros and companies/vendors. The Spiceworks community has a **Follow** function for both other IT pros and companies/vendors that interest you. You just search the community, find their page, and click on the **Follow** button. In the following screenshot I have included a user that is well known in the Spiceworks community and would be a great person to follow:

Here is an example of a vendor page with the **Follow** button highlighted:

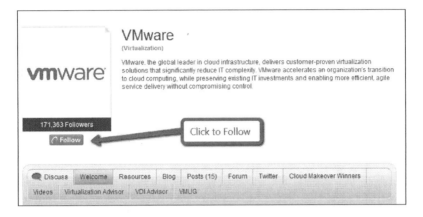

Now we all know the reasons to follow a fellow IT pro. What you may not know about following a company or vendor in the Spiceworks community is that many actually bring awesome content to their vendor pages instead of just fluff. Whether it be different methods (advisors) to determine what the best approach to starting a project with a new technology or actual tools to help you in your daily job. The vast majority of vendors on the community are there to help you out.

SpiceCorps and meeting other IT pros in your area

The community doesn't just do virtual connections. There are local user groups called **SpiceCorps** all over the world that get together and talk about issues they are having. Now, if you think that Spiceworks is all these folks talk about, you are very much mistaken. Even though everyone in the room is a user of Spiceworks, there is usually a presentation and round table discussion on general IT issues that folks are having a problem with and need a solution. As a new user to Spiceworks, these are great ways to meet some of the other Spiceworks users in your area. Now, to find one of these in your corner of the world, you could search the community for SpiceCorps. But since I am all about hooking you up, here is the link: http://community.spiceworks.com/spicecorps.

Once you get to that page, just put in your zip/postal code and country, and hit **Search**. The closest group will come up in the results. Now, if there isn't a group close to you, don't worry, you can start one! Every SpiceCorp out there has been started by a local user. If there is a group close to you, just click on the link and you can follow the group the same way as IT pros and vendors.

Other groups in the Spiceworks community

Besides local user groups, vendor pages, and users, there are a ton of other forums and pages in the Spiceworks community that can help you out. There are groups for just about every conceivable IT topic. When you find a forum that you either have expertise in or interests you, there is a Subscribe button so you can get updates when there are new posts. Here are a couple that you might want to check out.

The virtualization group

Who doesn't use some sort of virtualization in today's IT world? This group is a great resource for anything relating to virtualization. Virtual desktops, server virtualization, application virtualization, or even storage virtualization, this group has it all.

Check out the following screenshot and you can get there by typing this into your browser:

```
http://community.spiceworks.com/virtualization
```

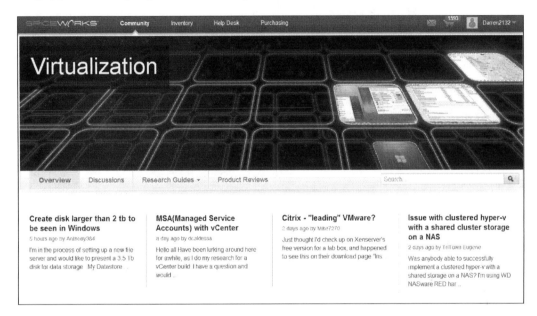

The mobile group

Mobile computing is one of the fastest growing segments of technology today. Whether it be tablets, phones, or the "next big thing" that is coming out, the mobile group covers it all. If you have specific questions on a device, you can find answers in the mobile group's forums that cover specific brands, mobile OSs, and even devices. Here is a screenshot and to get there, just type in `http://community.spiceworks.com/mobile` in the browser of your choice:

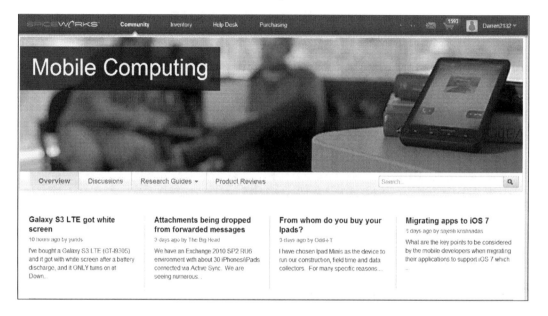

These are just two of many. If you have an interest or need a question answered, just do a quick search for groups and there should be one there waiting for you.

So go ahead and search the community for some individual IT pros (you have two that you already know), products you are using or are interested in, and a local SpiceCorp, and click on that **Follow** button! Go ahead and search for some groups or forums that interest you as well. You can do that now, this book is not going anywhere until you are finished.

All right! Now we are right where we want to be with getting you involved in the community. You should have your profile all set, set your privacy settings, and are following some IT pros/vendors/SpiceCorps/groups/forums. Nice job!

Now, with 567 individual forums, there is probably one out there for any topic you can think of (both IT related and non-IT related). We are going to focus on a couple of them that you can get immediate benefit from, specifically Spiceworks extensions.

Spiceworks extensions in the community

As we talked about earlier, Spiceworks is not open source. That said, the company has welcomed extension development with open arms. These extensions don't just come from users, many vendors have integration into the Spiceworks platform and have plugins to do a myriad of functions that Spiceworks doesn't do out of the box.

Luckily for us users, Spiceworks has all these extensions in one handy place so you can get them easily:

```
http://community.spiceworks.com/extensions
```

Or, you can just mouse over the **Community** link at the top of any page in your Spiceworks install and click on the **Extensions Center** link under the **Spiceworks** column.

The **Extensions** page you land on is pretty full of information. At the top, you will see the four main categories:

- **Plugins**
- **Reports**
- **Scripts**
- **Language Packs**

Let's look at each one of these sections.

Plugins

Now, Spiceworks is an awesome tool to make your IT day easier. That said, no tool does everything out of the box we need it to do; especially the one that is free. When users have found something that they needed within Spiceworks that wasn't included, they started writing plugins to do those tasks. Spiceworks saw this and made it really easy to install these plugins into your local install of Spiceworks.

To find some plugins, just click on the **Plugins** link on the Spiceworks **Extensions** page. Easy as that. This will take you to the main **Plugin** page. At the time of writing, there were 290 separate plugins; so to narrow things down a bit, there is a category list on the left of the page.

Help desk, inventory, user portal, and remote support are all here along with many more. In each category, there are four tabs on how you can sort the plugins: **Featured**, **Recent**, **Top Rated**, and **Top Downloaded**. The **Top Rated** list can be a little deceiving as a plugin with two ratings can have 5 stars and those that have 1,000 can have 4.5 stars. Not to say that a plugin with 2 ratings is going to be bad, but at this point in your Spiceworks journey, let's stick to some of the tried and tested ones. There are columns with how many times the plugin has been downloaded and how many ratings it has gotten as well, so you can tell which ones are newer and which ones have been around for a while.

Let's pick one out and walk through the process of adding it into your local Spiceworks installation. You are going to have to be on a computer that can directly connect to your Spiceworks install for this to work, though.

Since I know you will be using your user portal, let's get a plugin that will help you tweak it! Hmmm. There just happens to be a plugin called **Portal Tweaks**. Lucky for us! You can do a quick search for it or just enter the link `http://community.spiceworks.com/plugin/47`.

Once you get to the **Plugins** page, you will get the following screenshot:

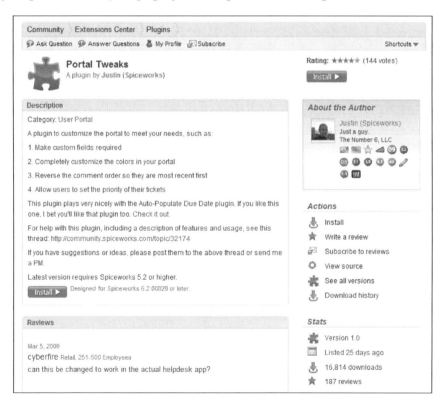

You can see the title, who wrote the plugin, description, reviews, and stats on this page. Many plugins also have screenshots to illustrate what changes they make to Spiceworks.

Now let's get to the complex process of installing it to your local Spiceworks environment. Do you see the orange **Install** buttons? Click on it. That's it. Can't get any simpler than that.

Whenever you install a plugin, it will automatically take you to your local Spiceworks plugin page. That way you can see all the plugins you have installed and uninstall any that you are not using or don't want. Pretty cool, right?

Go ahead and search for a few more plugins to install. I guarantee there will be something that you can use out there!

The last thing we are going to talk about is just a link. As you get more proficient with Spiceworks, you might have an idea for a fantastic plugin. Why don't you share your most excellent idea with the rest of the Spiceworks community? What to learn and how to write plugins? Just follow this link:

`http://community.spiceworks.com/help/Creating_Plugins`

Go ahead and have a read, and try to write one of your own. The Spiceworks community thrives on users like you who get involved!

Reports

We went through how to run and download reports in *Chapter 4, Configuring Other Spiceworks Features*, but we did not cover sharing reports directly into the community. If you have written a fantastic report, share it with others!

Now, if you have created an awesome report that you think will benefit other Spiceheads out there, sharing with the community is easy. Once you have created and saved the report, just click on the **Actions** drop-down menu and choose **Share**.

A window will pop up confirming you want to share the report and then Spiceworks uploads the report to the community. You are taken to the report page on the community where you can edit the description. Just a note on uploaded reports, just the report is uploaded, none of your data.

Scripts and Language Packs

The **Extensions Center** page has two more sections within it. The **Scripts Center** page is all about automating IT tasks. Users have uploaded scripts in PowerShell, VBScript, and even Batch and Bash. A bit of warning here, Spiceworks doesn't check the content of these scripts, so you might want to be careful. That said, if you are fluent in scripting, the code is displayed so you can see what it does. By using some of these great scripts, you can cut some precious minutes from your day.

A Language Pack allows Spiceworks to be run in a different language, basically translating Spiceworks into a local dialect. Did you know that many users have written Language Packs for Spiceworks? Yup, that's right. Clicking on **Language Packs** brings up the multitude of different ones that users have completed.

Real-world Spiceworks events

Local user groups are not the only real-world events that Spiceworks users attend, here are a couple of other examples of a bunch of crazy Spiceworks users getting together and having a great time.

Spiceworks University

Do you want to learn even more about Spiceworks? Well, Spiceworks introduced their Spiceworks University program in 2011. They have trainers that hold in-person training classes all around the United States and Europe. Not in either of those places? Not to worry, they have live webinars and are even rolling out on-demand learning. Their classes are focused on both basic (but you don't need that as you have this book) and more advanced topics, and are adding more all the time. If you are interested, check out the link `http://www.spiceworksuniversity.com` and the following screenshot:

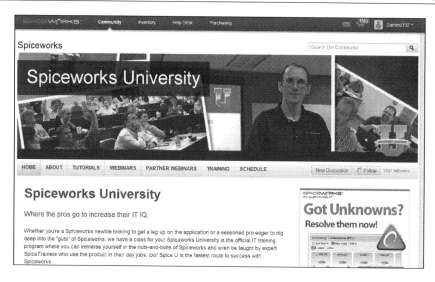

The SpiceWorld user conference

In 2007, Spiceworks was growing by leaps and bounds but still had a pretty small user base. They had a crazy idea. The idea was a two day Spiceworks user conference in Austin, TX. They weren't sure if anyone would show up, but it sold out. It has grown (and sold out) every year since. Where the first conference had general sessions, SpiceWorld today has so many breakout presentations on a variety of IT Topics (not just Spiceworks related). SpiceWorld was so successful in the U.S., they started in the U.K. in 2012. That sold out as well and they are having their second in 2013. Since we know you are loving Spiceworks, taking things to the next level would obviously be SpiceWorld! Here is the link `http://www.spiceworks.com/spiceworld`, and screenshot for more info:

Summary

In a nutshell, Spiceworks is what you make of it. There is a reason that more than 2.5 million IT pros have installed Spiceworks and so many of them are active on the community and attend in-person events. The community is a one-stop shop where you can get a report, answer a question, have a laugh, ask a question, get a quote, or install a plugin with just a couple of clicks. The in-person events are filled with great information and fun. The reason that Spiceworks has been successful is its users, and you are one of those now. So get involved and help to make Spiceworks even better than it is today.

So really, this last bit of knowledge we will impart to you is empowerment. Spiceworks empowers you, as an IT pro. It gives you tools to make your job easier and allows you to create even more. Not only that, but Spiceworks gives you an avenue to share what you have created with others. Remember this when downloading a report or plugin from another user, that they have been in the exact same situation you are in now—just having installed Spiceworks and excited about what comes next. The great thing about where you are right now is that you had this book to show you a few cool tips and tricks. As you work your way up the pepper scale and become a Spiceworks master, remember the folks who are just installing it for the first time. One of the reasons we wrote this book was to give something back to the many people who helped us along the way in our Spiceworks journey.

So, keep it spicy and we will see you on the community at a SpiceCorp or at SpiceWorld!

Index

Thank you for buying
Getting Started with Spiceworks

About Packt Publishing

Packt, pronounced 'packed', published its first book "*Mastering phpMyAdmin for Effective MySQL Management*" in April 2004 and subsequently continued to specialize in publishing highly focused books on specific technologies and solutions.

Our books and publications share the experiences of your fellow IT professionals in adapting and customizing today's systems, applications, and frameworks. Our solution based books give you the knowledge and power to customize the software and technologies you're using to get the job done. Packt books are more specific and less general than the IT books you have seen in the past. Our unique business model allows us to bring you more focused information, giving you more of what you need to know, and less of what you don't.

Packt is a modern, yet unique publishing company, which focuses on producing quality, cutting-edge books for communities of developers, administrators, and newbies alike. For more information, please visit our website: www.packtpub.com.

About Packt Open Source

In 2010, Packt launched two new brands, Packt Open Source and Packt Enterprise, in order to continue its focus on specialization. This book is part of the Packt Open Source brand, home to books published on software built around Open Source licences, and offering information to anybody from advanced developers to budding web designers. The Open Source brand also runs Packt's Open Source Royalty Scheme, by which Packt gives a royalty to each Open Source project about whose software a book is sold.

Writing for Packt

We welcome all inquiries from people who are interested in authoring. Book proposals should be sent to author@packtpub.com. If your book idea is still at an early stage and you would like to discuss it first before writing a formal book proposal, contact us; one of our commissioning editors will get in touch with you.

We're not just looking for published authors; if you have strong technical skills but no writing experience, our experienced editors can help you develop a writing career, or simply get some additional reward for your expertise.

Zabbix 1.8 Network Monitoring

ISBN: 978-1-84719-768-9   Paperback: 428 pages

Monitor your network hardware, servers, and web performance effectively and efficiently

1. Start with the very basics of Zabbix, an enterprise-class open source network monitoring solution, and move up to more advanced tasks later

2. Efficiently manage your hosts, users, and permissions

3. Get alerts and react to changes in monitored parameters by sending out e-mails, SMSs, or even execute commands on remote machines

Learning NAGIOS 3.0

ISBN: 978-1-84719-518-0   Paperback: 316 pages

A detailed tutorial to setting up, configuring, and managing this easy and effective system monitoring software

1. Secure and monitor your network system with open-source Nagios version 3

2. Set up, configure, and manage the latest version of Nagios

3. In-depth coverage for both beginners and advanced users

Please check **www.PacktPub.com** for information on our titles

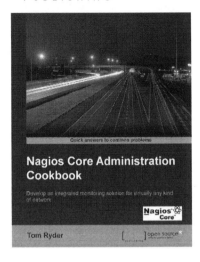

Nagios Core Administration Cookbook

ISBN: 978-1-84951-556-6   Paperback: 360 pages

Develop an integrated monitoring solution for virtually any kind of network

1. Monitor almost anything in a network

2. Control notifications in your network by configuring Nagios Core

3. Get a handle on best practices and time-saving configuration methods for a leaner configuration

4. Use the web interface to control notification behaviour on the fly and for scheduled outages, without restarts

Zenoss Core Network and System Monitoring

ISBN: 978-1-84719-428-2   Paperback: 280 pages

A step-by-step guide to configuring, using, and adapting the free open-source network monitoring system

1. Discover, manage, and monitor IT resources

2. Build custom event processing and alerting rules

3. Configure Zenoss Core via an easy to use web interface

4. Drag and drop dashboard portlets with Google Maps integration

Please check **www.PacktPub.com** for information on our titles

Made in the USA
San Bernardino, CA
20 May 2015